MAKING SCHOOLS WORK

MAKING SCHOOLS WORK

Improving Performance and Controlling Costs

Eric Hanushek

with

Charles S. Benson, Richard B. Freeman, Dean T. Jamison,
Henry M. Levin, Rebecca A. Maynard, Richard J. Murnane,
Steven G. Rivkin, Richard H. Sabot, Lewis C. Solmon,
Anita A. Summers, Finis Welch, and Barbara L. Wolfe

The Brookings Institution
Washington, D.C.

Copyright © 1994

THE BROOKINGS INSTITUTION

1775 Massachusetts Avenue, N.W., Washington, D.C. 20036

Library of Congress Cataloging-in-Publication data

Hanushek, Eric Alan, 1943—
    Making schools work : improving performance and controlling costs / by
Eric A. Hanushek with Charles S. Benson . . . [et al.].
      p. cm.
    Includes bibliographical references.
    ISBN 0-8157-3426-3 (cl.) — ISBN 0-8157-3425-5 (pbk.)
    1. School improvement programs—United States. 2. Educational
change—United States—Finance. 3. Academic achievement—United
States. I. Title
LB2822.82.H36 1994
371.2′00973—dc20
                                                    94-283225
                                                     CIP

9 8 7 6 5 4 3 2 1

The paper used in this publication meets the minimum requirements of the American National Standard for Information Sciences—Permanence of paper for Printed Library Materials, ANSI Z39.48-1984

Typeset in Times Roman

Composition by Harlowe Typography, Inc.
Cottage City, Maryland

Printed by R.R. Donnelley and Sons, Co.
Harrisonburg, Virginia

Preface

Schools need reform, on that Americans agree. Poverty, slow economic growth, growing budget deficits, and lagging international economic competitiveness are each linked to perceived shortcomings in the education and skills of American workers. Yet, although economic issues have driven the past decade's discussion of education reform, that discussion, surprisingly, has not included economic analysis of the reform proposals themselves.

The neglect of economic analysis is all the more surprising for the time and energy that economists have devoted to education and its relationship to the economy. Adam Smith's celebrated treatise, *Wealth of Nations*, published in 1776, stressed the importance of education to the performance of any economy. Since then economists have elaborated on Smith's observations that wealth flows from the productive powers of workers and that the skills and abilities that make up these productive powers are created by costly but worthwhile investments in education. With increasing precision, modern theoretical and empirical analyses have delved into all facets of schooling. The authors of this report are convinced that economic analysis of education reform deserves more attention, and this book therefore seeks to infuse a sense of economic reality into the discussion of education reform. The generally muted response of schools and national policymakers to calls for substantial change reflects, in our opinion, a broad failure of reformers on three counts: a failure to identify and deal with the costs implicit in the various reform proposals, a failure to create incentives for continuous educational improvement, and a failure to analyze and to monitor the effectiveness of new policies.

This project began when some members of what eventually became the Panel on the Economics of Educational Reform (PEER) held a preliminary meeting at the University of California at Los Angeles to explore the possible contributions of economics to ongoing discussions about educational reform. A somewhat surprising unanimity developed about not only the importance of economic principles to the debate, but also the outlines of an economic agenda for educational reform. Based on this, Eric Hanushek and Dean Jamison proceeded to discuss funding the project with The Pew Charitable Trusts and to set the basic framework. The original group was expanded to add expertise in a wider range of areas and to ensure balance in the Panel's general economic and political perspectives. Steven Rivkin provided analysis and support for the project throughout its development and, on the basis of his contributions, became a member of PEER. (The Panel mourns the death of Charles Benson, who participated in the project from its inception to the editing of the report.)

This effort has brought together a dozen economists from across the country who have been studying and reporting on various aspects of the educational system for at least a quarter of a century. Each has attempted in his or her professional career to bring economic analysis to bear on various aspects of education and schooling, an area of public policy that has traditionally eschewed such analysis. Collectively they provide a broad spectrum of views from within the economics community about education and educational reform.

The project called for each member of the Panel to prepare background materials on what is currently known about important aspects of education and its interaction with society and markets. The background papers are listed below and are linked to the text in the bibliographic notes for each chapter. The panel met on four separate occasions to debate how the various pieces come together and what it all means for policy.

Although economists are frequently known for their disagreements about policy prescriptions, both the broad outlines of the plan and the specific proposals elicited a resounding consensus in the PEER discussions. To be sure, various individuals place more weight on some interpretations than others, and none agrees with every word in this document. But the convergence of opinion about the central principles and conclusions was remarkable.

The Pew Charitable Trusts provided financial support and encouragement for this effort. Moreover, Robert Schwartz and Ellen Burbank, while representing Pew, went beyond purely financial support by participating in the final meeting and providing intellectual contributions to the panel.

Many colleagues and commentors have contributed to the ideas set forth here. In particular the Panel thanks Nabeel Alsalam, Stanley Engerman, George Farkas, John Jackson, Bruce Jacobs, Dale Jorgenson, John Kain, David Kirp, Daniel Koretz, Joe Nathan, Robert Strauss, David Weimer, John Witte, and Michael Wolkoff for offering helpful comments and suggestions on early drafts. Barry Goldstein provided research assistance. Jennifer Church edited an early version of the manuscript. John Browning offered editorial advice that substantially improved the structure of the manuscript. Martha Gottron provided the final editing, adding noticeably to the readability.

Bibliographic Notes

The history of economists' treatment of education can be found in Kiker (1968). Although many economists have been concerned with education, a very important early writer on education and the economy was Smith (1776 [1979]). Modern interest in economic aspects of education was rekindled by Schultz (1963) and Becker (1975).

Panel on the Economics of Educational Reform

Eric A. Hanushek: Professor of Economics and Public Policy; Director, W. Allen Wallis Institute of Political Economy, University of Rochester.

Charles S. Benson: Professor of Education; Director, National Center for Research in Vocational Education, University of California, Berkeley.

Richard B. Freeman: Professor of Economics, Harvard University.

Dean T. Jamison: Professor of Education and of Public Health, University of California, Los Angeles; Population, Health, and Nutrition Advisor, The World Bank.

Henry M. Levin: David Jack Professor of Higher Education and Economics; Director, Accelerated Schools Project, Stanford University.

Rebecca A. Maynard: Trustee Professor of Education and Social Policy, University of Pennsylvania.

Richard J. Murnane: Professor of Education, Harvard University.

Steven G. Rivkin: Assistant Professor of Economics, Amherst College.

Richard H. Sabot: John J. Gibson Professor of Economics, Williams College; Senior Research Fellow, The World Bank.

Lewis C. Solmon: President, Milken Institute for Job and Capital Formation.

Anita A. Summers: Professor of Public Policy and Management, Wharton School; Professor of Education, Graduate School of Education, University of Pennsylvania.

Finis Welch: Professor of Economics, Texas A&M University; Chair, Unicon Research Corporation.

Barbara L. Wolfe: Professor of Economics, Preventive Medicine, and Public Affairs, University of Wisconsin, Madison.

PEER Background Papers

Readers interested in specific background papers should contact individual authors.

Benson, Charles S., Maya H. H. Ibser, and Steven G. Klein. *Economic Returns to Vocational Education and Other Types of Occupational Training.*

Hanushek, Eric A. *Notes on School Finance 'Reform.'*

Hanushek, Eric A., and Richard Sabot. *Notes on Changes in Educational Performance.*

Lau, Lawrence J., and Jong-Il Kim. *Human Capital and Aggregate Productivity: Some Empirical Evidence from the Group-of-Five Countries.**

Levin, Henry M. *The Economics of Educational Reforms for the Disadvantaged.*

———. *Economics of Educational Time.*

Maynard, Rebecca, and Eileen McGinnis. *Policies to Meet the Need for High Quality Child Care.*

Murnane, Richard J. *Evidence on Teacher Supply and Directions for Policy.*

Rivkin, Steven G. *Residential Segregation and School Integration.*

Sabot, Richard, and Richard Freeman. *Test Scores and Labor Productivity.*

Solmon, Lewis C., and Cheryl L. Fagnano. *Business and University Collaboration with the Schools.*

Solmon, Lewis C., and Steven G. Rivkin. *The Demography of American Education into the Next Century.*

Summers, Anita A., and Amy W. Johnson. *A Review of the Evidence on the Effects of School-Based Management Plans.*

Wolfe, Barbara L., and Sam Zuvekus. *Nonmarket Outcomes of Schooling.*

*Commissioned paper.

Contents

CHANGE: Economically Realistic Alternatives for Education in the Twenty-First Century

Tables

Figures

Text Boxes

SUMMARY

Making Schools Work: Basic Principles

Economic issues motivate the movement to reform America's schools. Despite ever rising school budgets, student performance has stagnated. Disappointing student performance, in turn, contributes to disappointing economic growth, stagnating living standards, and widening gaps among the incomes of different social and ethnic groups. Yet, although economic issues are central to the problems of education, economic ideas have been notably, and most unfortunately, absent from plans for reform. This report attempts to redress the balance by presenting a plan for education reform that incorporates economic principles.

The report represents the efforts of a panel of economists to bring economic thinking to school reform. The panel concludes that school performance can be improved, without increasing expenditure, through a reform program guided by three broad principles—efficient use of resources, performance incentives, and continuous learning and adaptation. Although perhaps obvious in the stating, these principles are notable in their absence from discussions of school reform.

—*Efficient use of resources.* Educators must strive consistently to use the available financial and human resources to maximize student performance. Too often in the education debate, the meaning of efficiency has been twisted into something unpleasant and counterproductive. Efficiency does not mean a relentless, single-minded drive to cut costs. Nor does it mean reducing education to an assembly-line routine based on procedures certified as "efficient." What it does mean is that educators should measure both the costs and benefits of various approaches to education—and choose the approach that maximizes the excess of benefits over costs in their particular circumstances. Today, by contrast, the benefits of new plans are often assumed rather than systematically measured, and little effort is made to compare the potential net benefits of programs competing for limited resources. Bad programs are allowed to continue, siphoning off resources that could be productively employed to improve student performance.

—*Performance incentives*. Educators and students, at all levels of the school system, should be rewarded for actions that improve student performance. Education is too complex an endeavor to manage by rote, or, as is often attempted today, by curricula and rigid rules handed down from state and local boards of education. These agencies fail to recognize that teachers and other local decisionmakers inevitably have great leeway to improve or reduce school efficiency. Performance incentives that reward them for progress toward the goals of the schools—while recognizing their freedom to determine how that progress is best achieved—are the best way to focus teachers, principals, and other school personnel on improving education. To create such incentives, schools must define both goals and measures of progress toward those goals more clearly than they have yet done. That task will not be easy. But it is necessary. Without clear goals and measures, the success of any school reform is more luck than design.

—*Continuous learning and adaptation*. Schools must learn systematically from their experience. No matter how successful or unsuccessful current reform programs are, schools will always face the challenge of improving. Yet schools today have no real mechanisms or procedures for managing that continuous process of improvement—for discovering which programs work and which do not, for promoting the good ones and weeding out the bad. Other fields of human endeavor, notably business and medicine, are engaged in continuous experimentation, developing new approaches to the challenges that face them. Schools, we believe, must follow suit. At the very least, better management of the innovation that now occurs in schools can prevent one community from repeating the failures of its neighbors.

Unlike most existing programs of school reform, our approach cannot be distilled into a single curriculum or program of education that promises to cure the ills of today's schools. Indeed, we doubt that a single answer exists. Instead we describe a process of continuing reform, a procedure for finding and eliminating inefficiencies and for discovering and disseminating improvements. By adopting the economic principles on which this approach is based, American schools can begin to find effective answers to the many problems that they face. Schools structured around these economic principles—such as the Accelerated Schools program for disadvantaged students now instituted in some twenty-five states—have demonstrated that academic performance can be improved while costs are controlled.

Some have argued that schools are too important to be subject to economic rigor. We argue that, on the contrary, they are too important not to be. Only by working diligently to improve themselves can schools fulfill the trust placed in them by the nation.

Why Worry about Schools?

Schools produce huge benefits for America. For individuals, schooling increases earning power and helps them obtain such intangible goods as health and happiness. For society as a whole, schools foster the productivity improvements that drive economic growth, inform the dialogue of democracy, and reduce the gaps of understanding and income dividing the groups that make up the nation's diverse society. But evidence is mounting that in recent years the costs of education have been growing far more quickly than the benefits. From this observation springs the impetus for reform.

After allowing for inflation, the amount spent on each pupil in America's schools has increased unabated for a century, with

Figure S-1. Real Current Expenditure per Student, 1890–1990

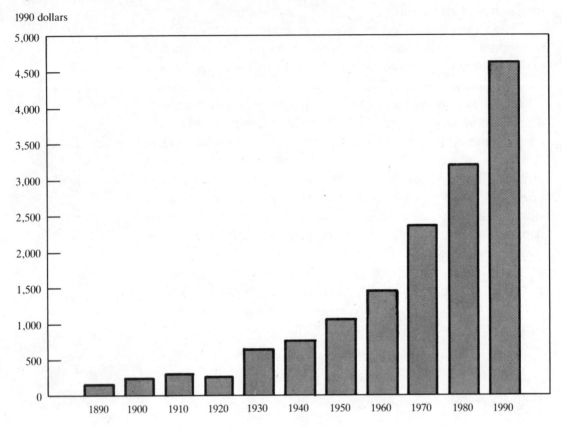

1990 dollars

SOURCE: Hanushek and Rivkin (1994).

steady growth at almost 3.5 percent a year (figure S-1). During the past three decades, however, student performance has, at best, stayed constant and may have fallen. Achievement on science exams, shown in figure S-2, is depressingly representative of the performance pattern for the population as a whole and for its major racial subgroups. As the performance of American students has stagnated, students in other nations have caught up or surpassed them. Comparisons of U.S. and Japanese students in the early 1980s showed, for example, that only 5 percent of American students surpassed the average Japanese student in mathematics proficiency. America's future no longer can be guaranteed by expand-

Figure S-2. Science Achievement of Seventeen-Year-Olds, by Race and Ethnicity, as Measured by the National Assessment of Educational Progress, 1970–92

Average scale score

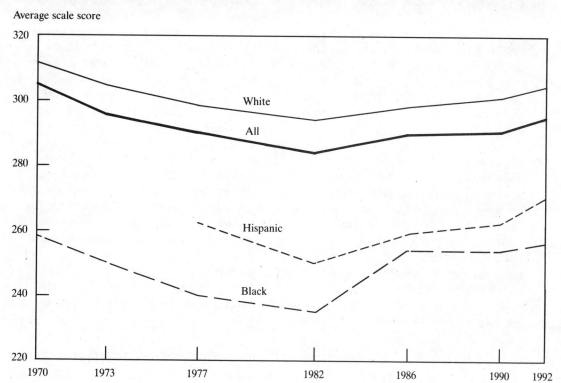

Source: U.S. Department of Education (1993).

ing the amount of schooling its population receives but instead depends on the quality of its schools. But that quality is lagging.

In addition to academic woes, a fiscal crisis looms for America's schools. During the 1970s and 1980s the student population fell dramatically. Aggregate spending on schools thus rose much more slowly than per-pupil expenditures, because declines in the overall student population offset increases in per-pupil spending. But the student population is rising again. Prospective expenditure increases are likely to collide with public disappointment in stagnant school performance—and taxpayers may well resist future expenditure increases with unprecedented insistence.

Box S-1. A Glossary of Key Terms

Although this report is written for others besides economists, we have needed to use several specialized terms. A few of these require careful explanation, because they are general terms with a specific meaning here and because they are frequently misunderstood.

—**Efficiency** means, in simplest terms, doing the best possible with the resources at hand. If a new process improves student performance and costs the same as the one being used, the new process is more efficient. If a new process produces the same student performance as the one being used but costs less, the new process is similarly more efficient. But efficiency does not mean, as it is sometimes interpreted, simply reducing costs. If both costs and performance are reduced by a new approach, it is not necessarily more efficient. Efficiency also must be based on acceptable and full measures of student performance, not just narrow measures such as test scores or dollars. Pursuing efficiency does not prejudge what schools should be producing.

—**Evidence,** as used in this report, is reserved for conclusions drawn from systematic, scientific investigations of schools. Everybody has personal opinions about schools, but these individual, anecdotal observations can be very misleading. A key feature of this work is identifying ideas and results that have stood up to extensive scrutiny and that are supported by data from schools.

—**Performance incentives** are rewards and punishments related to the achievement of

Worse, many of the most popular school reforms have raised costs without increasing student performance. Studies show that reducing class size usually has no general effect on student performance, but because teacher compensation is already the schools' biggest single expense, smaller classes and commensurately more teachers raise costs dramatically. Nevertheless, states and local districts doggedly try to reduce class sizes. Similarly, a good deal of evidence shows that advanced degrees do little to ensure that teachers do a better job in the classroom—while they do enable teachers to command higher salaries. Yet more and more states are requiring teachers to obtain advanced degrees as a prerequisite for entering the profession. The problem is not that school administrators disregard the evidence, but simply that they never see it. A system to measure the effectiveness of education programs is seldom incorporated into school administration or into state and local policymaking.

specific outcomes. Incentives may be promised in advance, such as those written in teacher contracts, or given more spontaneously, such as giving a teacher a choice classroom assignment after a successful year. Incentives may also be monetary (such as year-end bonuses for bringing all students in a class up to grade level in reading) or intrinsic (such as the praise a teacher gets from colleagues for doing a particularly good job). Extensive research confirms that teachers, like others in society, adjust their behavior in accordance with the incentives they face. This research also confirms that incentives have a stronger effect on behavior the more explicit and well defined they are—and the larger the perceived rewards. Accountability, as typically defined, is a special form of performance incentive where people are held responsible for outcomes; often, however, only minimum levels must be met.

—**Value added** is a shorthand term signifying the contribution of schools, programs, or specific teachers to learning. Students start school with some knowledge and cognitive skills developed at home, through friends, or from previous schooling experiences. Students also differ in individual ability. Value added represents the school's unique contribution to a student's knowledge and skills, after taking into account these other sources of learning. Performance incentives and evaluations of school programs must focus on value added to eliminate possible distortions from other educational influences.

Needed Changes

Today school reforms are often sold on the basis of prospective benefits alone. Costs are not considered, nor are costs or benefits systematically measured after the programs are in place. One reason that schools find performance so difficult to improve is that they often do not know how well they are doing in the first place. We believe this situation must change and that educators and students alike must focus on improving performance. We further believe that better performance is best accomplished by the introduction of well-crafted incentives.

Effective incentives require clear definitions of good performance. These definitions in turn require agreement on the goals and objectives of the schools. In the past developing such definitions has proved difficult and contentious. Although we cannot offer an easy solution to the political difficulties of defining a good education, performance in core academic areas should be paramount. Moreover, it should be measured by a broad array of indicators—and not by narrow, standardized tests alone.

Although many of the ideas underlying new programs of educational incentives are conceptually appealing, little practical experience has accumulated. Somewhat hesitantly, schools have begun to experiment with a wide variety of incentive structures. These systems differ both in how they define "good" performance and in how they reward it. Charter schools and merit schools enable teachers to set up new schools to try out new educational ideas. School choice and educational vouchers allow students and their parents to determine whether schools are good or not by deciding where to attend. Merit pay for teachers and principals and contracting educational services to private firms provide still other performance definitions and incentives. The existing applications have been very limited, nonetheless, making generalizations from them impossible.

Worse, little effort has been made to evaluate these innovative programs when they have been applied or to disseminate knowledge about their results. If schools are to build up the knowledge on which to base reform, a broad program of experimentation and evaluation is necessary. Progress in medicine has been greatly speeded by systematic experiments to test the efficacy of new treatments and to disseminate knowledge about their success or failure. A similar program of innovation could benefit schools.

In general terms, all of the promising incentive programs involve decentralized decisionmaking to capture the energy and imagination of the educators and students in each school. But these incentive programs differ in a crucial way from the programs of "site-based management" being implemented in many schools to decentralize decisionmaking. Much of the current movement treats decentralization as an end in its own right, irrespective of performance objectives. Incentive programs, however, by focusing decisionmaking on student performance, make decentralization a means for improving that performance.

The educational problems of the disadvantaged are frequently treated in an entirely different way from more general reform, but we believe this separation is largely inappropriate. The average performance levels of disadvantaged students in this country are undeniably low, and society must follow through on its general commitment to eliminate these disparities. But, while programs for the disadvantaged may differ from programs for other students in the details—for example, by trying harder to involve families in education or by coordinating better health and nutrition programs—the most effective approaches will be based on the same principles as more general reform. Careful attention to student outcomes, the development and institution of performance incentives, the evaluation of programs, and attention to both costs and benefits must be central to any plan for improving the education of disadvantaged students.

Altered Roles

Concern about effective use of school resources, emphasis on incentives, and recognition of the importance of evaluation are far from the organizing themes for today's schools. Moving to such a system, with the extensive experimentation that it will necessarily entail, will require the participants in education to take on quite new roles and responsibilities.

In many ways teachers are the most important element of the schooling system, and they must take an active part in developing better schools. Their improved participation will be encouraged, even demanded, by schools focused more clearly on student performance. Yet teaching under new systems of education based on performance incentives and decentralized decisionmaking promises new challenges and requires experience, training, and expectations different from those required today. Care must be taken to balance the need for change with the realities of today's schools. Two-tier employment contracts, for example, are one useful method for introducing changes into teaching while minimizing the risk of alienating the existing teachers, who will remain a substantial portion of the total teacher force for many years to come. Under such systems, new teachers would receive different contracts from existing teachers, contracts that generally involve fewer tenure guarantees, more risks, and greater flexibility and rewards. The second tier of the contract permits existing teachers to continue under existing employment rules for tenure, pay, and work conditions unless they choose to be covered by the new contract. Other strategies for inducing existing teachers to participate in new systems of education are also available and should be actively explored.

State governments also must change their role substantially. Instead of regulating education by laying down the curricula and procedures that schools must follow, the states should promote and encourage local experimentation with new systems, aid in implementing new incentive systems, and help produce and disseminate information about new programs and their results. States need to define performance standards and explicit goals for students to reach. States share with the federal government a responsibility to ensure equality of opportunity. Disadvantaged students may well require additional resources, even when all schools are using resources effectively. Moreover, states must monitor the performance of local districts and intervene when local performance falls to unacceptably low levels. Such intervention need not, and should not, take the form of threats either to replace local districts with state personnel or to impose new curricula and procedures dictated from state level. Instead the most useful interventions will probably help the students of poorly performing districts to help themselves, through school choice programs or voucher systems that will enable them to move to better schools elsewhere. These new roles entail radical but essential departures from the focus of current state policy. Without venturing into these different and uncertain areas, efforts at improvement will be crippled, if not completely thwarted.

The federal government should take a primary role in fostering goals and standards of academic achievement, developing performance information, supporting broad program evaluation, and disseminating the results of evaluations. The federal government should also take primary responsibility for ensuring equality of opportunity for all citizens, but especially disadvantaged and minority students. This may, for example, involve expansions of early childhood education, integrated health and nutrition programs, and other interventions to supplement background disadvantages. These roles are consistent with many of the federal government's current functions, but a central consideration in adopting any such supplemental program is how it complements the emphasis on performance proposed for schools. If supplemental programs for the disadvantaged and minorities are to achieve their purpose, they must be subject to the same principles of decisionmaking as are general school reforms.

Local school districts should take new responsibility for setting curricula, managing teaching and administrative personnel (including hiring and firing on a performance basis), and establishing closer links with businesses (particularly for students not continuing on to postsecondary schooling). Although none of these differs from local current tasks, each would be significantly different in content if states removed many of their restrictions on instruction and organization. Moreover, if major decisions devolved to local schools, new emphasis would be placed on management and leadership.

Businesses also have new roles. Although businesses have frequently lamented the quality of workers they receive from schools, few have ever worked closely with schools to define the skills and abilities that they are seeking in prospective workers. More direct input to schools, perhaps coupled with long-term hiring relationships, could aid both schools and businesses. Moreover, businesses could provide students with valuable incentives to perform well in school by making it clear that they base hiring decisions on detailed examination of school transcripts. Today most businesses seem to disregard, more or less entirely, transcripts and other evidence of a student's academic accomplishments. Finally, business managers might have much to teach schools about the effective use and management of performance incentives, for they have much experience that schools lack.

As has long been recognized, parents have a central role in providing their children with high standards, positive attitudes and behaviors, and the motivation needed for success. These continue.

But a new focus on schools is added. Although parents often have few opportunities to play an active role in schools today, they have a crucial part in many incentive-based systems of school management. Systems of school choice require parents to decide which school offers the best opportunities for their children. Systems of decentralized management offer parents a chance to participate in the running of schools and indeed may require it. Effective governance of schools relies on the indispensable feedback of the schools' clients.

An Overriding Perspective

After painting a beguiling description of how new programs should be introduced, new activities undertaken, and bright new futures realized, it is traditional for those proposing new school reforms to plead for more funding. Here we break with tradition. Reform of schools will best be achieved by holding overall real expenditure constant. Schools must learn to consider trade-offs among programs and operations. They must learn to evaluate performance and eliminate programs that are not working. They must learn to seek out and expand upon incentive structures and organizational approaches that are productive. In short, they must be encouraged to make better use of existing resources.

Inefficiencies in the current structure of schools are widespread, but interest or pressure to eliminate them is scant. Where there is interest, it is often thwarted by regulations or contract restrictions that do not permit reasonable adjustments in personnel, classroom organization, the use of new technologies, or other approaches that might improve performance at no additional expenditure. The basic concerns of economics, with its attention to making expenditures effective and to establishing appropriate incentives, must be used if schooling is to improve.

Economic discipline cannot be imposed blindly. We recognize that variations in local circumstances, cases of special need, and start-up costs for new programs may require additional finance.

But poor performance is certainly not an automatically convincing case for more money. Quite the contrary.

In the long run the nation may find it appropriate to increase school expenditure. It is simply hard to tell at this point. But expanding resources first, and looking for reform second, is highly unlikely to lead to an improved system—a more expensive system, certainly, but one with better performance, unlikely.

1

The Urgency of a Well-Focused School Reform

Americans agree on the need for school reform, but that consensus is not matched by a consensus on the best approach for reform. If reform of the schools is to be effective, policymakers must face up to three fundamental economic tenets: the costs and benefits of any specific program or approach must be weighed against those of other possible reforms; organizations that function well establish clear incentives for good performance; and serious evaluation of performance is a prerequisite to ongoing improvement. In describing and documenting our plan to address these fundamental realities, we draw on the considerable amount of information available about what does and does not work in schools, information that has not yet been mobilized to forge the innovative systems the nation needs.

Interest in school reform is not new. A long history of dissatisfaction with public schools forms the backdrop for today's efforts. Not long ago the Soviet Union's launch of Sputnik convinced many that America's schools were falling behind in a global competition. Although the Soviet Union no longer exists as a country, concern about our schools remains—albeit in somewhat different form. The pressures of developing the technological and scientific underpinnings needed to compete globally were augmented in the 1960s and 1970s by a desire to provide equal schooling opportunities for the poor, the handicapped, and disadvantaged children in general.

Neither concern has gone away. As we will document, the students coming out of America's elementary and secondary schools fare poorly in head-to-head competition with students from many other parts of the world—even though per-student expenditures on schooling in the United States have historically exceeded those of every other country. Further, the schools have been unable to bring all students up to acceptable levels of achievement, leaving a long-term disadvantaged group that most likely will be unable to participate in the American dream of enjoying an ever improving standard of living.

Recently a new concern has emerged. During much of the post-Sputnik debate over schools, the nation held a lunar-landing conception of reform: devote sufficient energy and resources to the problem, and the nation will crack it. But actual experience in the nation's schools is shaking faith in this conception. Despite the increasingly large amounts of resources devoted to schools, student performance has shown few tangible improvements. Indeed, more and more people concerned with the high cost and seemingly low return of additional spending in the educational system are joining those with traditional concerns about performance and equity to urge immediate reform.

Pressures on the Schools

Students, parents, taxpayers, and politicians—virtually everybody linked with schools—now call for schools to do a better job. The news media regularly report the failures of American education, from American students' poor showing in international test score competition to individual examples of graduates who have difficulty coping with specific tasks in the workplace. These continual, often shrill demands for improvement have obviously made themselves felt on school personnel and decisionmakers, creating ongoing pressures on schools.

But, even while calls for better performance continue, schools are asked to take on new and difficult obligations. The school has been identified as the institution that must deal with drug problems, adolescent health issues, crime, and violence. Even if schools are not explicitly assigned these new responsibilities, their task has implicitly expanded as support for students from traditional sources outside the classroom declines. The increases in the numbers of single-parent families, working mothers, immigrants with deficiencies in English, and children in poverty conspire to make the educational task of schools more challenging. These pressures require schools to work harder simply to stay in the same place.

Perhaps greater resources might overcome these problems, but school funding is already bumping against limits. Education faces stiff competition for society's limited resources. The federal government's budget deficits place particular constraints on finance for new program activities. State and local governments also face intense competition for resources—without the option of deficit financing. The current fiscal squeeze at all levels of government implies that any significant expansion in funds for new activities is unlikely without offsetting cutbacks in some other area, and easy places for cutbacks have long since disappeared.

Even staying in the same place in fiscal terms may be difficult for education. The ever increasing demands for additional health care funding, for example, cut into money available for schools. Other people, similarly, have trumpeted the value and importance of infrastructure investments by government. The list of alternative uses for public and private funds is long. Simply arguing that education is a productive activity does not and should not ensure that schools will continue to receive even the same funding as they currently do.

Maintaining the current quality of teachers is also becoming more expensive for schools. The wages of college-educated workers, particularly college-educated females, have grown substantially during the past few decades and are likely to continue to grow. So schools will have to pay more to attract teachers of the caliber of those that they now employ. At the same time, the declining student enrollment of the past decades has ended and is now reversing. So schools will also need more teachers.

Herein lies the policy challenge: how to overcome public discontent with the performance of schools at the same time that school responsibilities, costs, and competition for resources are increasing. Given these real conflicts, it is understandable that school personnel, students, and their parents may be dissatisfied and discouraged. The conflicts also underscore why nobody should believe that there are quick or easy answers to the problems of schools.

Motivation for This Study

None of these observations of schools' ills is new. Awareness of the problems has already led to a spate of reform reports and proposals. Indeed, a 1983 report, *A Nation at Risk,* started a virtual avalanche of investigations into American schools, an avalanche that has continued unabated for a decade. Why then produce another study?

A fundamental shortcoming of existing discussions of school policy has been the lack of coherent consideration of economic issues. Few of the reform proposals have even addressed the costs implied by the changes they suggest, let alone attempted to compare costs to benefits.

This lack of attention to costs is understandable. Many of the reports have taken the perspective that the most important initial step is to gain public support for schools. Talking about costs does not gain support—quite the contrary. Ignoring costs, however, does not help the nation to face up to the reality that massive increases in the funding of education are unlikely to occur, particularly if the performance of the educational system remains impervious to improvement. Despite significant additional resources for education during the past quarter century, student achievement has shown no clear growth. Moreover, neither strong economic recovery nor change in political leadership seems likely to promote continued high growth in funding for public schools. Thus the cost implications of proposed improvements are central, unavoidable concerns.

Ignoring efficiency is also understandable. Existing proposals for school reform give short shrift to notions such as efficiency and incentives, in part because they have negative connotations. Some assume that making efficiency a goal for school policy is synonymous with minimizing costs. Others conjure up images of narrow-minded bean-counting, which distorts the goals and operations of the educational system. Incentives are often viewed as a plot by outsiders to interfere with the activities of the teaching professional.

These views reflect misconceptions about incentives and efficiency goals, and ignoring these issues could have dire consequences for American education. The nation is past the time when mobilization of the public is needed. Public awareness of the need for significant changes in the schools exists. The issue now is what kind of changes are best.

We are persuaded that widespread use of appropriately designed performance incentives will bring positive results without large budget increases. Ample evidence can be found throughout industry and society to demonstrate that individuals respond to well-structured incentives. In a wide variety of circumstances, organizational objectives are better met through performance incentives than through regulations and administrative directives.

Indeed, lack of proper performance incentives may explain why education appears to lag behind many other sectors in its ability to harness the drive and ingenuity of its workers. There is no clear relationship between the performance of teachers and schools and the incentives and rewards that they are offered. We believe that innovative teachers and principals are the key to student achievement but that the structure of incentives currently works to inhibit and constrain them.

The design of effective performance incentives requires considerable information both about the educational process, including potentially efficiency-enhancing new technologies and techniques, and about how individuals are likely to react to different incentives. Additionally, differences in local circumstances, history, and goals are likely to produce extensive variation in the details of successful incentive programs. Because of these local differences, careful planning is needed in designing and evaluating these programs. But many existing reform proposals simply ignore information about their likely effect. Policy proposals now offered and introduced in schools are much more likely to be based on current popularity than on any hard data derived from experience. Documentation is not always available, of course, but existing proposals frequently neglect what is available. This oversight is unfortunate because, not infrequently, the evidence strongly suggests that a popular proposal is unlikely to achieve its stated goal.

Perhaps because evaluation has played such a minor role in past school reform, most proposals do not provide for ongoing evaluation and accumulation of knowledge about the effectiveness of different plans. If there is to be a coherent program of improvement, learning from experience is indispensable.

In sum, we believe that the school reform discussion has neglected a series of important issues. Effective public policies cannot be made without recognizing the economic trade-offs that are involved. A hesitancy to bring hard choices out in the open may explain in part why reform seems to be so slow in coming.

A Critical Juncture

School reform is at a critical juncture. Dissatisfaction with schools, from virtually all quarters, presents an opportunity to make fundamental changes. But the public is unlikely to continue to tolerate poorly conceived reform programs, ones that lead merely to calls for additional reform. Badly structured reform will dampen public enthusiasm and willingness to undertake changes. Therefore, it is important to settle on the right course from the start.

Moreover, demographic factors make the 1990s a decade of unusual opportunities. A majority of current teachers will leave the profession during this period. Many of the reforms that we believe to be sensible involve significant changes in the organization of schools, in the expected behaviors and rewards of teachers and other school personnel, and in the overall characteristics of the teaching profession. New teachers are likely to be more receptive to these changes because they will not regard the new policies as violations of past understandings or intrusions on their accustomed routine. Potential teachers could apply for teaching positions based on their willingness to accept different work rules and activities, and they could participate in developing the new programs of which they will be a part.

At the same time, the growth in the student population that is just now beginning will put added pressure on school finance. Taxpayers, frequently unhappy with the results of past increases in school spending, are unlikely to look kindly on new money demands, even if they are driven solely by demographic forces. So schools will be forced to alter their past spending patterns. The results of this process will be much more satisfactory if schools are prepared to introduce new efficiency into the educational process.

The United States with and without Educational Reform

The potential benefits of school reform are large. Without reform the nation will become noticeably poorer. Investment in education has a high return, and passing up such investment is costly, especially over the long term. Better schools could be an important determinant of whether the United States is able to sustain a high rate of economic growth. Recent investigations of economic development suggest that, although the nation might be able to achieve short-term productivity improvements by diverting money from education to other kinds of investments, education plays a special role in supporting high, long-run growth.

Nonetheless, the case for education should not be overstated. Education is but one of many potentially worthwhile investments. Only by considering costs and benefits together—both short-term and long-term—can the nation hope to choose wisely among its opportunities.

Unlike most other areas of potential investment, our schools are demonstrably inefficient. Inefficiency here means simply that the nation devotes more resources than needed to achieve the current level of student performance, or, conversely, that it is not achieving as much as it could with the resources currently devoted to schools. Inasmuch as potential savings exist, school performance can be improved without additional money. This potential for improving the return on investment distinguishes schooling from other areas of possible investment, such as plant and equipment or infrastructure.

Finally, schools have occupied a unique position on the policy agenda because improvements in schools might simultaneously achieve two goals: improved productivity and more even chances of success for all in society. Enhanced investment in educating the children of the poor has been central to policies for reducing poverty. Any policy that improves the nation's economic base could provide the resources for improving the distribution of economic well-being, but few alternatives are as appealing, or as politically acceptable, as improving individual education and training.

A Unique Viewpoint

We strongly believe that reform should be based on current overall spending levels. Plans to introduce new programs or policies should not include simultaneous appeals for new funds and resources. This is a unique perspective on educational reform, one that is at odds with all other reform proposals.

Why do we take this position?

First and foremost, we believe that the educational system must develop a disciplined approach to decisionmaking, one that includes automatic and ongoing evaluations of programs, personnel, and operations. The promised benefits of new programs should be judged against their costs, and only the most cost-effective programs should remain on the reform agenda. Existing programs also should be judged by their benefits and costs, and the programs that offer the least net benefit should be phased out. The benefit-cost yardstick must be applied to both old and new programs if improvement is to be ensured.

Because current operations are so inefficient, additional resources can be found by making better use of current funds. Although it is not possible to judge accurately how much could be gained by improving today's operations and although the amount clearly varies across local school systems, there is no question that sizeable overall inefficiencies currently exist. The possibility of tapping into poorly used resources makes budget-neutral reform less constraining.

Our belief in budget-neutral reform is not a dogmatic statement of political philosophy. Instead, it is a conclusion, documented below, that flows from our analysis of today's schools and of how they got to where they are—and how they can get to where they should be.

Two caveats to this operating principle deserve mention. First, program start-up costs present a special situation. Because developing and implementing a program entail genuine, one-time expenses, special allowances should be made. In particular, constraints on initial funds should not be allowed to impede the flow of ideas and innovations. Second, special problems of some specific school systems, often systems serving disadvantaged students, require attention. This is not meant to be a blanket statement, because many of the school systems currently judged to be substandard are in fact spending well above the national average, and general fiscal and educational mismanagement, when that is the core problem with performance, should not be rewarded with additional funds. In education the claim that lack of resources is the major factor limiting performance appears to be vastly overused and frequently demonstrably untrue.

Budget-neutral reform does not preclude future increases in educational resources. Such increases should, however, await the evidence of success of reforms. The remainder of this study lays out recommendations on how to proceed.

THE CONTEXT

Economic Performance of the Existing System

2

The Economic Returns from Educational Investment

Education has fueled the growth of the U.S. economy. Schooling has expanded dramatically during the twentieth century, increasing the skills of the labor force, which form an important part of the nation's wealth. Schools have helped individuals to take on new occupations and to rise to new levels of income and social status. For all of its importance, however, the role of schools should not be oversold. Education is ultimately an investment and thus is best evaluated alongside other, perhaps more mundane, forms of capital spending such as roads and machinery. Education is a high-return investment, but it is not the only high-return investment opportunity available. Achieving a sensible policy toward schools requires a thoughtful and balanced consideration of the costs and benefits of schooling. Overselling the value of schools—perhaps by representing them as an investment in human potential morally beyond the reach of cost-benefit analysis—ultimately causes as many problems as underselling it.

Education has historically been thought of simply in terms of the amount of schooling that an individual has attained. This convenient yardstick has been used, for example, to track overall changes in the skill of the labor force and has permitted direct analysis of the economic value of different amounts of schooling. But there is growing appreciation that simply measuring the quantity of schooling attained does not account for differences in schooling. Individuals with the same years of schooling can have widely differing skills and cognitive abilities. Today, the important decisions about schools relate largely to quality differences in the knowledge and abilities of individuals.

The Pattern and Importance of Schooling

Economists view schooling as an investment both by individual students and by the society at large. Both incur costs and both reap rewards. For a student, the costs of education include any direct, out-of-pocket costs, such as tuition, books, and other school-related expenditures, as well as the "opportunity cost" of the income that the student forgoes when attending school instead of taking a paying job. In return the student expects better labor market opportunities and other improvements in well-being.

In a similar fashion, society incurs direct costs in subsidizing a public school system that provides free education to millions. It also forgoes the opportunity to devote to other projects the skills, people, and resources that are engaged in education. In return society expects a more productive labor force, a better-informed electorate, and a better-functioning society in general. For both the individual and society, the profitability of any investment is determined by comparing benefits and costs. Regarding education as an investment underscores two key criteria for evaluating educational decisions. Benefits must be directly compared with costs. And the profitability of any specific investment must be compared with alternative investments. These are themes we will return to throughout this report.

A look at the history of the twentieth century suggests that schooling has generally been a good investment. Individuals have dramatically increased their own investments in education. At the turn of the twentieth century, only 6 percent of the adult population had finished high school. After the First World War high school graduation rates began to increase rapidly. But changes in education work their way only slowly through the overall population. By 1940 only half of Americans aged twenty-five or older had completed more than eight years of school—that is, had had any high school education at all. Not until 1967 could the United States

Figure 2-1. Median Years of Schooling by Age, 1940–90

Years of school

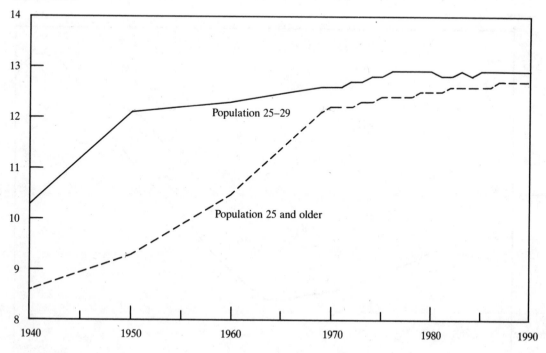

SOURCE: Snyder (1992).

boast that half of its citizens aged twenty-five or older had completed high-school.

Since 1967 the rate of increase in the number of years of schooling has slowed dramatically. The young adult population, aged twenty-five to twenty-nine, has had stable completion rates for almost two decades (figure 2-1). Today, the median years of school completed by Americans aged twenty-five and older—that is, the number completed by at least half of the population—stands at slightly less than thirteen years.

The benefits of education to individuals are clear. The average earnings of workers with a high school education remain significantly above those of the less educated, and the earnings of workers with a college education now dwarf those of the high school educated. The earnings of college-educated workers,

Figure 2-2. Ratio of Earnings of College and High School Graduates: Young White Workers, by Sex, 1966–90

Relative weekly wages

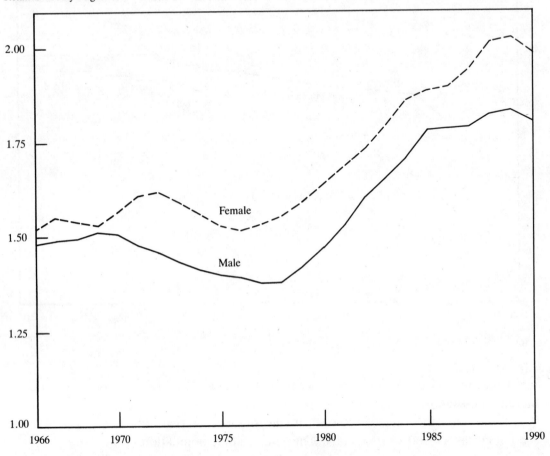

SOURCE: Author's calculations from U.S. Bureau of the Census, *Current Population Survey*.

charted in figure 2-2, are now more than 70 percent higher than earnings of high school graduates with similar job experience. College-educated workers also enjoy greater job opportunities and suffer less unemployment. High technology economies seem to have a voracious appetite for skilled workers, who can adapt to new technologies and manage complicated production processes effectively. So for individuals, at least, the increased relative incomes of more-educated people have been sufficient to offset the costs, making additional schooling an attractive investment.

Individuals also reap nonfinancial benefits from education. For example, more-educated people make better choices concerning health, according to the evidence, so they tend to live longer and to have healthier lives. Evidence also shows that the children of more-educated parents get more out of school. They attend longer and learn more. These benefits of schooling reinforce those from the labor market.

Society as a whole also benefits from education. The nation is strengthened economically by having workers with more and better skills. National income rises directly with individual earnings (which are a major component of national income). Moreover, recent economic studies argue that education may provide economic benefits to society that are greater than the sum of its benefits to individuals; by providing a rich environment for innovation and scientific discovery, education can accelerate the growth rate of the economy. The more educated are more prone to vote in local and national elections, and a better-informed and more responsible electorate improves the workings of a democratic society. Increases in the level of education also are associated with reductions in crime.

Education has also helped to achieve both greater social equality and greater equity in the distribution of economic resources. Schooling was, quite rightly, a centerpiece of the War on Poverty in the 1960s, and the benefits of improved schooling are demonstrated in comparisons of the earnings of different social and ethnic groups. Earnings by blacks and whites have converged noticeably since the Second World War, and much of this convergence is attributable to improved educational opportunities for African Americans. Providing an exact accounting for the benefits of education to society is difficult, because many of the benefits education provides are hard to value. But for our purposes it is safe to say that education historically has been a good investment both for society and for individuals.

School Quality

Why, then, today's debate over education if the evidence suggests it has been a good investment? For most of this century, policy deliberations focused on the amount of school attained—school completion rates, the proportion of the population attending post-secondary schooling, and the like. Analyses of the benefits of schooling were most concerned with the effects of quantity of schooling, as measured by changes in individual incomes or other important matters, such as the number of people who voted. Recent events, however, have combined to shift the focus of the policy debate to the quality of schooling, rather than the quantity.

As the growth in the number of years that Americans spend in school virtually stopped, so did many of the benefits that Americans might have expected from a continuously growing educational system. Income growth has slowed, and children no longer routinely surpass the earnings of their parents. Income convergence between blacks and whites also has stopped—coincident with a slowing in the convergence of the schooling completion rates for the two groups.

At the same time, increasing global competition requires the United States to judge its educational achievements not just against its own past, but also against the current achievements of other nations. Nations around the world have increased their levels of schooling dramatically, with high school completion rates in several competitor countries now rivaling those of the United States. Thus, America can no longer be sure that its work force is of higher quality than that of its trading partners.

Both of these new realities shift the focus of the educational debate from quantity to quality. By itself, the amount of schooling attained proves to be an imprecise and potentially misleading measure of the level and distribution of individual skills. Moreover, it neglects some central elements of the policy debate. Specifically, improving the quality of schooling, or how much is learned each year, has been seen as away to counteract the effects of the U.S. slowdown in the growth of quantity of schooling.

The reason for questioning American education, its past successes notwithstanding, is straightforward. Improving quality of education does not appear to be making up for the slowdown in the growth of schooling; on the contrary, declining quality may be making things worse. Data from a variety of sources suggest that the knowledge and skills of American students are not as high as they once were or as they are now for students in other nations. Moreover, it costs much more to achieve today's lower levels of student performance than it did to obtain the higher levels of the past. The next chapter examines and documents these assertions in more detail; here we concentrate on the links between student performance and their own success and that of the economy.

The economic effects of differences in the quality of graduates of our elementary and secondary schools are much less understood than the effects of quantity, particularly with regard to the performance of the aggregate economy. The incomplete understanding of the effects of educational quality clearly reflects difficulties in measurement. Although quality of education is hard to define precisely, we use the term to mean the knowledge base and analytical skills that schools are intended to instill in their students. Measurements of school quality, including those that are incorporated into research, tend to be much narrower, frequently coming down to such things as performance on a specific standardized test. This narrow assessment is unfortunate. Many researchers and decisionmakers rightfully question whether individual standardized tests adequately measure the relevant skills, and many object to relying on existing tests as the only measure of quality. Even if quality differences are very important for subsequent success, they argue, specific, narrow measures are unlikely to capture the full importance of such differences and may even distort the picture of how quality differs across schools and over time. Nevertheless, mounting evidence suggests that observed differences even in these limited measures of student performance are increasingly important indicators of performance in the workplace.

Research on differences among workers as measured by performance on cognitive test suggests that individual variations in performance are significant in determining incomes. Although early estimates of differences in income attributable to differences in cognitive achievement tended to be rather modest in magnitude, evidence now suggests that the effects of cognitive differences may have grown over the past decade and a half. Differences in cognitive skills, especially mathematical and analytical skills, seem to be very important in determining subsequent success, particularly for those directly entering the labor market from high school. Further, cognitive performance of individuals is known to have a very strong effect on attendance and completion of college. The far greater earnings attached to a college education suggest that cognitive performance has a clear and strong indirect effect on labor market performance. Thus, differences in cognitive skills, even narrowly measured, appear important in determining economic and labor market success for the individual.

The link between individual cognitive skills and aggregate productivity growth is much more difficult to establish. There is no clear consensus on the underlying causes of improvements in the overall productivity of the U.S. economy nor on how the quality of workers interacts with economic growth. One observation is useful, however. Productivity growth continued at some 2 percent a year through the 1960s but fell off to 1 percent a year in the 1970s and then to virtually zero in the 1980s. Noting that these productivity changes mirror the aggregate pattern of a decline in scholastic test scores (see the next chapter), some have gone on to presume that the apparent decline in educational quality revealed by the test scores was driving the productivity changes. That could not be the case, however, because those with lower test scores remained a small proportion of the total labor force through the 1980s. Lower test scores in the 1980s may signal forthcoming problems, but they cannot explain recent changes in the economy.

Even if the decline in educational quality has not yet affected economic performance, various signs suggest that the potential impact is well worth examining. For example, surveys of employers invariably indicate an increasing dissatisfaction with the workers they can hire. Employers cite their shortcomings not only with simple skills such as reading ability, but also with more complicated tasks such as reasoning ability and quantitative skills. These subjective impressions are confirmed by more objective measures, including recent investigations of adult literacy. Part of this seemingly growing dissatisfaction could result simply from new demands on workers—such as the need for line workers to be able to calculate statistical quality measures—instead of an actual decline in abilities. Part could result from a snowballing of dissatisfaction heightened by the media. But such repeatedly voiced concerns demonstrate once again how quality has moved to the center of the debate over education.

Some Cautionary Views

Education has helped to make this "the American century." Although neither theory nor econometric analysis has found any simple relationship between improvements in the skills of individuals and overall gains in the productivity of the labor force, available estimates generally suggest an important role for schooling in productivity growth. But other kinds of investment equal or surpass education's contribution, a point that is often obscured by the rhetoric of educational reform. Capital investment has been extraordinarily important. New technologies and new ways of producing goods and services have made firms and factories increasingly productive. Rising productivity directly increases the standard of living. Although invention and technological change are surely related to education, it would be wrong to argue that education is the whole story or that innovation justifies all investments in education.

As with productivity, so with international trade: education is only a part of the large and complicated story of the U.S. trading performance. The eclipse of American cars, consumer electronics, steel, and textiles, among other industries, by foreign competition is taken as evidence that American industry is losing ground in international competition. Often the latest bad news on trade brings forth comparisons of foreign and American workers. Yet the American work force remains more educated overall than the competition, even though other countries are rapidly closing the gap. To repeat, however, the narrowing international gap in both the quantity and quality of education may signal future problems, but it cannot explain the already observed changes in trading relationships. A variety of factors, including natural endowments, existing plants and equipment, access to technology, organization of markets and firms, and the quality of the work force, govern the pattern of production and trade among nations. Changes in comparative advantage occur regularly in the natural course of economic evolution.

Some people are upset to find that foreign countries can now produce various technologically advanced goods that formerly were the exclusive province of the United States. Others are concerned about the political implications of shifting economic strength. But the United States has never had a monopoly in goods with a high skill component, and it continues to develop patents, license products, and export items that involve a significant input of skilled labor. A better-educated U.S. work force would clearly affect the kinds of goods the United States had a comparative advantage in producing and change some of the trade patterns. Yet, equally clearly, even the best-educated U.S. work force is unlikely to regain its position in a wide variety of industries, from basic metals such as steel to many high-tech items. The education of the labor force changes only very slowly and is but one element in determining the course of international trade. Educational investments will not turn around all of the history of international trade changes. Nor will they lead to immediate and dramatic changes in productivity growth and the level of national income.

Overselling the value and potential impact of education has two dangers. Investments made in pursuit of exaggerated benefits may divert resources from other, ultimately more beneficial, alternatives. More pragmatically, repeated disappointments from overselling education's benefits could eventually discredit the whole idea of educational investment.

Continued investment in education can, according to existing estimates, have significant effects on the U.S. economy. But that does not necessarily hold for any investment in education. The investments must lead to performance improvements, or quality gains, by students. With the end of expansion in overall schooling levels, full attention must be focused on improving the knowledge and skills of youngsters going through the schools.

Bibliographic Notes

The recent pattern of returns to further schooling can be found in Murphy and Welch (1989, 1991) and Kosters (1991). School dropout rates and completion are analyzed in McMillen and others (1993). The discussion of nonmarket returns to schooling is based on Barbara Wolfe's background paper. Further information on those issues can be found in Michael (1982) and Haveman and Wolfe (1984).

The consideration of how education relates to economic growth and aggregate productivity is found in Lucas (1988), Romer (1990), Barro (1991), Jorgenson and Fraumeni (1992), and World Bank (1993). A comprehensive review of the varied effects of education on growth and productivity is found in Sturm (1993).

The discussion of school quality and earnings relies on the background paper by Richard Sabot and Richard Freeman. Specifics related to the economic returns to vocational education come from the background paper by Charles Benson, Maya Ibser, and Steven Klein. Recent analyses include Bishop (1989, 1991), Murphy and Welch (1992), and Murnane, Willett, and Levy (1993). The relationship between measured schooling and school quality attributable to changing patterns in GED (General Educational Development credentials) completion is analyzed by Cameron and Heckman (1993). The discussion of distributional issues including earnings differences by race, relied on, among others, Smith and Welch (1989), O'Neill (1990), Juhn, Murphy, and Pierce (1991), Bound and Freeman (1992), Card and Krueger (1992a, 1992b), Grogger (1992), and Levy and Murnane (1992).

3

Rising Expenditure, Falling Performance

Many popular accounts of schools suggest that they have changed little over the past few decades—except perhaps that students have gotten worse. This popular conception, however, misses truly extraordinary changes, not only in the organization and governance of schools, but also in the resources devoted to them. Even a cursory examination of the historical patterns of student performance and school finance highlights a central mystery of the education debate. The nation is spending more and more to achieve results that are no better, and perhaps worse. The standard nostrum of educational reformers— that additional resources should be devoted to each student's education—belies the fact that per-pupil spending has increased steadily throughout the century. If a case is to be made for increasing educational expenditure, analysis must first begin to understand why past increases in spending are not now producing increased quality. This chapter begins that analysis by tracing the history of public educational expenditure and student performance.

The History of Overall Cost Growth

Many of the calls for educational reform emphasize the need for renewed commitment to schooling, which often translates into an appeal for expanded resources for schools. Accompanying this appeal is an apparent belief that real educational spending (that is, the amount spent after accounting for inflation) has been constant or has even fallen. Others acknowledge increases but point to the growth in special education or spending on administration to explain why growing expenditure might coincide with declining quality. But data prove these assertions wrong. Such errors are potentially dangerous, because without a good understanding of how today's education dollar is spent, it is hard to see how to devise schemes for more effective spending tomorrow.

By some measures expenditure on education has grown faster than spending on health. Yet while health care costs are the subject of vigorous debate, the unremitting growth in educational spending receives only passing attention in most policy discussions. More ironic, when attention does focus on education expenditure, it is usually to suggest that spending should rise. But educational expenditure has risen strongly and steadily in real terms throughout the century. Some of the increase is a simple consequence of the increased numbers of school-aged children, but a larger part reflects active policy choices to increase the amount spent on behalf of each student by hiring more and higher-paid teachers to teach smaller classes.

Real public expenditure on elementary and secondary education in the United States rose from $2 billion in 1890 to almost $190 billion in 1990. (All monetary measures are adjusted by the gross national product—GNP—deflator to constant 1990 dollars; educational expenditure excludes capital costs.) This almost hundredfold increase was more than triple the GNP growth rate during the same period. Educational expenditure increased from less than 1 percent of GNP in 1890 to more than 3.5 percent of GNP in 1990.

Spending on public schooling as a percentage of GNP actually peaked in 1975, at almost 4 percent, when baby boomers reached their maximum school-going years. But demographics are only the lesser part of the story of rising educational spending. Rising per-student expenditure explains the bulk of the change in educational outlays. Figure 3-1 plots increases in per-student expenditure from

Figure 3-1. Real Current Expenditure per Student, by Instructional Staff and Other Expenditures, 1890–1990

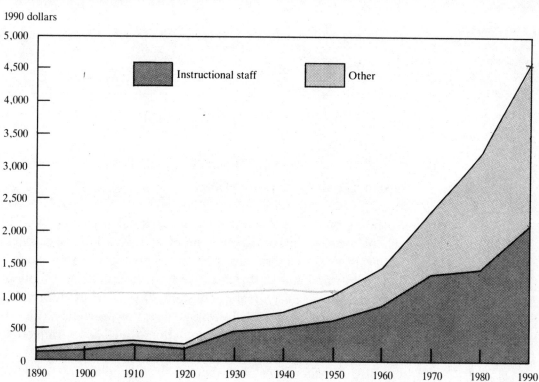

1990 dollars

SOURCE: Hanushek and Rivkin (1994).

1890 to 1990. Real per-student expenditure rose from $164 in 1890 to $772 in 1940 and to $4,622 in 1990, roughly quintupling in each fifty-year period. The figure also separates spending on instructional staff—mainly salaries for teachers and principals—from other school spending. Today, expenditure on instructional staff accounts for roughly 45 percent of total school spending. In 1940, by contrast, it accounted for about two-thirds. (Even though instructional staff spending excludes items directly related to classroom activities, such as teacher retirement costs, books, and materials, this division does approximately track the locus of spending between the classroom and elsewhere.)

Table 3-1. Factor Contributions to Growth in Spending on Instructional Staff, 1890–1990

Percentage

Factor changes	1890–1940	1940–70	1970–90	1890–1990
School population[a]	34	38	−35	29
Instructional intensity[b]	23	22	85	28
Teacher cost[c]	43	40	50	43
Total	100	100	100	100

SOURCE: Hanushek and Rivkin (1994).

a. Combined effect of changes in the size of the school-age population, the school enrollment rate, and the rate of public school attendance.

b. Combined effect of changes in the pupil-teacher ratio and the number of school days a year.

c. Effect of changes in the price of teachers.

Instructional Staff Expenditure

Spending on instructional staff is perhaps the key component of school costs. It determines how many and what kind of teachers are available for classroom instruction. Three factors drive spending on instructional staff (which we frequently refer to simply as teachers, although a roughly constant 10 percent of the total is spent on other instructional personnel such as principals). First is the absolute size of the school population, which is determined by the numbers of children of the relevant ages, by whether they are enrolled in school, and by whether these schools are public or private. The second factor is variation in the intensity of instruction—including varying average class sizes and the length of the school year. The third force is wage rates and other personnel costs, primarily for teachers. Table 3-1 illustrates how these three separate forces have affected the growth in instructional staff expenditure over the past century.

In the early period (1890–1940), a rapidly increasing school-aged population and a rising public school enrollment rate accounted for roughly one-third of the $11.5 billion increase in real instructional staff expenditure. The school-aged population grew by 13.6 million, the enrollment rate rose from 68.4 percent to 80.7 percent, and the percentage of students attending public schools increased by three percentage points to slightly more than 90 percent. Slightly more than 25 million children were enrolled in the public school system by 1940, double the number in 1890.

Even during this period of rapid population growth, however, increases in the amount spent on each student accounted for two-thirds of the rise in instructional staff expenditure. Most of this increase in per-student expenditure came from a rise in the price of teachers, which increased by a factor of 2.5 and which, by itself, explained more than two-fifths of the growth in total expenditure. Changes in the length of the school year and in the pupil-teacher ratio accounted for almost a quarter of the expenditure increase. The average school year lengthened by forty days, and the pupil-teacher ratio declined by roughly 20 percent, from thirty-five students per teacher in 1890 to twenty-eight students per teacher in 1940.

Between 1940 and 1970 increases in the public school population continued to push total instructional staff spending up. Public school enrollment again almost doubled, accounting for 38 percent of the increase in real spending. Most of this increase followed directly from growth in the school-age population, but the overall school enrollment rate rose by five percentage points during this period, to 85.8 percent, while the proportion of students attending public schools fell by two percentage points, to just below 89 percent. By 1970, 46 million children were enrolled in public elementary and secondary schools.

As in the period before 1940, increasing intensity of instruction accounted for something over a fifth of the expenditure increase between 1940 and 1970. But, because the length of the school year had stabilized by 1940, almost all of this increase was the result of a declining pupil-teacher ratio. That ratio fell to twenty students per teacher during this thirty-year period, a drop exceeding both in absolute numbers and percentage terms the decrease of the previous fifty years. The rising price of instructional staff again accounted for about two-fifths of the expenditure increase. Teacher wages nearly doubled in real terms over the period, increasing from $83 a day in 1940 to $155 a day in 1970.

Changes in costs between 1970 and 1990 differed dramatically from the two earlier periods. Because of falling birth rates, public school enrollment fell to 41 million students in 1990, roughly 5 million students less than in 1970. Yet continuing rapid growth in per-student spending increased aggregate real spending on instructional staff by 30 percent. The largest factor in expenditure growth was the further decline in the pupil-teacher ratio, which fell to under sixteen students per teacher in 1990. Increases in teachers' salaries also accounted for a substantial portion of the increase in per-student expenditure. Between 1970 and 1990, teacher price increases were almost 50 percent greater than the total cost savings from the reduced quantity of school children. But the increases were far from uniform. Between 1970 and 1980 the average price of teachers declined by more than $10 a day, as teachers' earnings failed to keep up with the high inflation rates. Then between 1980 and 1990 teachers' real wages jumped by more than $40 a day.

One contributing factor in the decline in the average pupil-teacher ratio might be an increase in the number of difficult-to-educate children, such as handicapped children or children from low-income families. But the general nationwide decline in the pupil-teacher ratio, which occurred across schools in communities with a wide variety of student populations, suggests that this is not the fundamental reason for change. Direct analysis, discussed below, confirms this conclusion.

Two additional observations, which will be discussed in a subsequent chapter, compound the puzzle of public perceptions concerning school expenditure. First, according to substantial evidence, variations in student-teacher ratios do not strongly affect student performance. Second, variations in pupil-teacher ratios do not seem to represent a policy response to changes in the costs of teachers. Whether prevailing wages go up or down for college-educated workers, the student-teacher ratio continues to decline. For these reasons, declining student-teacher ratios would seem to be a pure cost increase that does not lead to improved performance or greater efficiency. Thus these expenditures on reducing student-ratios directly lower the return on any educational investment.

Historical analysis of spending changes may help to explain why public perceptions of school expenditure diverge so signifi-

Figure 3-2. Annual Growth in Real Spending, 1890–1990

Percentage

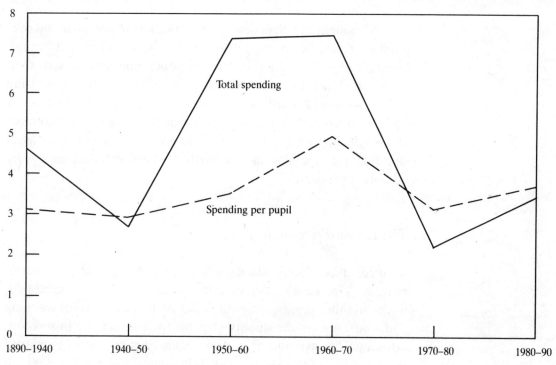

SOURCE: Hanushek and Rivkin (1994).

cantly from the facts. During the last two decades the drop in the school-age population masked many spending changes. Between 1970 and 1990 the decrease in the student population offset a substantial portion of the increase in instructional costs. So total spending (and the tax rates required to cover spending) rose much less than did real spending per student. Figure 3-2 shows the annual growth rates for total spending and for per-pupil spending from 1890 through 1990. Interestingly, except for a period of high growth during the 1960s, average growth in real spending per pupil has been relatively constant at 3 to 3.5 percent a year. But the pattern for total spending, which is affected

31

directly by changes in the student population, has been much more erratic, ranging from slightly more than 2 percent to more than 7 percent a year.

Although total spending grew noticeably slower than did per-pupil spending between 1970 and 1990, the situation is changing. During the 1980s the fall in student population first slowed, then reversed. Data on school enrollments since 1990 confirm that rising school populations will add to aggregate expenditure instead of subtracting from it. The result could well be rising popular concern about educational expenditure—and a much more difficult fiscal situation for schools—as the myth of constrained spending by schools is exposed.

The Rising Price of Teachers

Changes in teachers' salaries affect more than the cost of education. Any increase or decrease in teachers' wages compared with wages in other sectors alters the relative attractiveness of teaching and, thus, affects the quality of people who enter the profession. Although the average daily wage of instructional staff increased from $34 in 1890 to $83 in 1940 and to more than $183 in 1990 (all expressed in real 1990 dollars), teachers' earnings have generally declined relative to other similarly skilled workers.

The pressure of increased costs of teachers on overall school expenditure is to be expected. Schools must compete with other industries for highly skilled workers. But other industries have experienced much more pronounced productivity gains than have schools, allowing these industries to bid more for the workers they want. To attract teachers of the same quality year after year, schools must raise their salary offers, which adds to school expenditure. Alternatively, schools could refuse to keep up with the wages offered elsewhere and let the quality of people they recruit slip.

Figure 3-3 compares the average earnings of teachers to those of other college graduates who did not enter teaching. Specifically,

Figure 3-3. Percentage of College-Educated Workers Earning Less than the Average Teacher, by Sex, 1940–90

Percentage

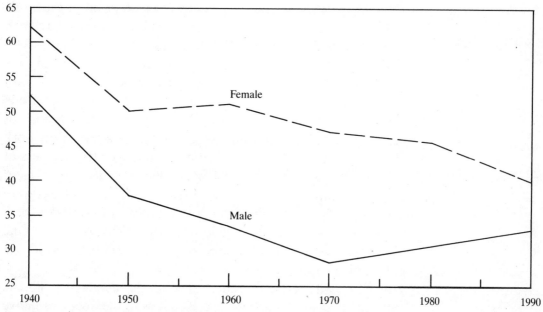

SOURCE: Hanushek and Rivkin (1994).

it charts the percentage of other college graduates earning less than the average teacher. The data are also standardized to allow for differences in the age distribution of teachers and nonteachers. A low percentage means that teaching is relatively less attractive. The general picture is one of declining attractiveness for teaching. The increases in teachers' wages did not keep up with the increases in salaries for college-educated workers in other sectors. Had the overall earnings of teachers kept pace with other careers between 1970 and 1990, the price of teachers would have risen by an additional four percentage points.

Moreover, changes in the relative attractiveness of teaching have differed considerably between men and women. For men the decline in the attractiveness of teaching was most dramatic in the 1940s, with a steady but less sharp fall continuing through 1970.

In 1940 the average male teacher earned above the median for college graduates employed elsewhere. By 1960 only one-third of those outside teaching were earning less than the average teacher. The relative attractiveness, however, reversed again in the 1970s and 1980s as male teachers by 1990 regained the same relative position they held in 1960.

By contrast, average earnings for women in teaching remained close to the median earnings in outside employment until 1960, when relative earnings for female teachers began to erode steadily, followed by a sharp decline in the 1980s. Because of rapidly expanding opportunities for women elsewhere in the work force (see figure 2-2), the decline in the relative attractiveness of teaching did not reverse itself in the 1980s, as it had for men. Although more than 40 percent of female college graduates were teachers in 1970, only 19 percent were in 1990. More starkly, only 11 percent of female college graduates ages twenty to twenty-nine were teaching in 1990, compared with 41 percent of the same age group two decades earlier.

Although the best teachers may not be the people who can earn the most in other jobs, direct analysis of the data on relative earnings indicates that most college graduates at the top of the ability distribution are entering fields other than teaching and that outside earnings opportunities strongly influence the choice to enter and to remain in teaching. Indeed, the perennial shortages of teachers in mathematics and the sciences result largely from the greater earnings opportunities that technically trained people can find outside of schools.

It is the recent decline in the relative earnings of women teachers that holds the greatest potential problems. For better or worse, the financial attractiveness of teaching for men has changed little or even improved for the past two or three decades. For women, however, changes are more recent and continuing. Because women account for roughly two-thirds of elementary and secondary teachers, the decline in relative earnings potential may well cause significant future problems in attracting and retaining skilled teachers.

The Cost of Special Education

One frequently cited explanation for increases in educational spending is the growth in numbers of mentally and physically handicapped students, coupled with legal requirements for providing educational services for them. But, despite significant growth in special education, new programs for the handicapped appear in fact to have played a relatively minor role in both the growth in spending and the decline in pupil-teacher ratios.

Concerns about the education of children with physical and mental disabilities were translated into federal law with the enactment of the Education for All Handicapped Children Act in 1975. This act prescribed a series of diagnostics, counseling activities, and services to be provided to handicapped students. To implement this and subsequent laws and regulations, school systems expanded staff and programs, in many cases developing entirely new administrative structures. The general thrust of the educational services has been to provide regular classroom instruction—"mainstreaming"—where possible, along with specialized evaluation and instruction to deal with the specific needs of the handicapped.

The availability of extra funding for those students deemed handicapped creates incentives for school systems to expand the population of special education students. The availability of intensive teaching and specialized programs creates similar incentives for parents. Although public school enrollment declined by more than 3 million students between 1977 and 1990, the number of public school students classified as disabled increased by 25 percent, from 3.7 million to 4.6 million, raising the percentage of students classified as disabled from 8.5 percent to 11.4 percent of total public school enrollment. The number of special education teachers increased even faster than the number of children classified as disabled, rising by more than 50 percent between 1978 and 1990.

Simple calculations demonstrate that special education could account for less than one-third of the recent fall in the pupil-teacher ratio. The ratio fell from 17.4 pupils per teacher in 1980 to 15.4 in 1990, a decline of more than 11 percent. But even if both the proportion of students classified as disabled and the pupil-teacher ratio in special education programs had remained constant, the aggregate pupil-teacher ratio would still have fallen to 16.0.

Research also suggests that the growth in special education explains only a small portion of the overall increase in educational expenditure between 1980 and 1988. Although the costs of educating each child vary greatly, the average per-pupil cost of special education has been estimated to be roughly twice the cost of educating a child who does not require any special education. If that is true, then the expansion in the special education population of the 1980s would have cost, at most, $3 billion, which is quite small in comparison with the aggregate expenditure increase of more than $54 billion during this period. Taken together, these analyses indicate quite clearly that growth in special education could account for only a small part of the growth in per-student expenditure in the 1980s.

Policies for the special education population emphasize providing extra services for the identified population in need, a population that previously was not assured of any distinctive services. There is no reason to believe that the proportion of students requiring such aid has changed over time, only that they now are more accurately singled out for particular services. Thus, the legislated services should, by lessening the burden of the handicapped on the classroom teacher, make regular classroom expenditure relatively more effective over time. In other words, increased spending for special education should also yield benefits for regular classroom instruction.

Other Expenditure

Despite vigorous growth, increased spending on instructional staff has been outpaced by growth in other sorts of educational spending. Such growth in other spending is often attributed to administrative bureaucracy. For example, former Secretary of Education William J. Bennett wrote, "Too much money has been diverted from the classroom; a smaller share of the school dollar is now being spent on student classroom instruction than at any time in recent history. It should be a basic goal of the education reform movement to reverse this trend toward administrative bloat and to reduce the scale of the bureaucratic 'blob' draining our school resources." Unfortunately the real picture is more complicated. "Other" spending, that is, spending other than that for instructional staff, has indeed been growing fast. But this statistical category includes teachers' pensions, health insurance, books, and classroom support staff that would arguably be more sensibly included under the heading of total instructional expenditure.

Overall, other spending grew from $0.4 billion in 1890 to $6.4 billion in 1940, and to $101 billion in 1990. Since 1960 this other expenditure per student rose at an annual average of 5 percent, compared with only 3 percent a year for instructional staff expenditure. The relative growth of other spending was most rapid during the 1970s, a period when the total school-age population dropped significantly. Few administrators (and few teachers and other school personnel) appear to have been let go when the student population dropped. Had all expenditure grown at the same rate per student as instructional staff expenditure between 1960 and 1990—a period in which the pupil-teacher ratio fell by a third—per-pupil spending in 1990 would have been less than $3,500. Instead the actual figure was more than $4,600 (in real 1990 dollars). In other words, had other factors simply increased in intensity at the same rate as instructional staff expenditure for the past three decades, total expenditure would be one-quarter less.

Sparse and inconsistent data make a full understanding of the growth in these other spending categories difficult. Table 3-2 uses available data to show the current distribution of educational expenditure. Until 1980, at least, the two fastest-growing expenditures in the other spending category were fixed charges and an expenditure called "other instruction," which includes books and school support staff. The bulk of fixed charges are payments for staff retirement and health insurance. So a substantial portion of the other spending category would actually seem to belong with the direct expenditure for instructional staff. The only category

Table 3-2. Percentage Distribution of Current Expenditures, 1960–90

Year	Instructional staff	Other instruction	Central administration	Maintenance	Fixed charges	Other	Total
1960	61	7	4	12	7	9	100
1970	57	11	5	10	10	7	100
1980	46	15	5	11	14	9	100
1990	46	12	a	42[a]	a	a	100

SOURCE: Hanushek and Rivkin (1994).
a. Costs for central administration, plant maintenance, fixed charges, and other spending are not separately available for 1990.

separately listed for administration is expenditure on central administration, which includes all administration that is outside of the individual school buildings, such as superintendents, central testing staff, curriculum development staff, and financial services personnel, but not principals. Central administrative costs have remained roughly 5 percent of total expenditure since the Second World War. Frustratingly, data available for 1990 are not comparable in detail with those for 1980. Although spending on "other instruction" declined as a share of total spending between 1980 and 1990, it is impossible to determine what happened to the other main categories of expenditure previously identified.

In pure staff terms, ratios of total staff to pupils have fallen even more rapidly than teacher-pupil ratios. There was a single staff person—teacher, administrator, clerical, counselor, or whatever—for every 19.3 students in 1950. By 1990 that ratio had dropped to 1 staff person for every 9.1 students.

Conclusions about Costs

Even if the student population had remained constant, real aggregate school expenditure would have increased twenty-five-fold over the past century. Three factors played crucial roles: the rising price of instructional personnel, the declining pupil-teacher ratio, and rising noninstructional staff costs. Although rising costs are often blamed on factors outside of the schools' control, such as mandated special education services, or on nonclassroom activities, such as increased central bureaucracy, there is little evidence that these are the primary forces driving up spending. Each plays a part but is dwarfed by other pressures for expanded spending.

The general lack of concern among reformers about the magnitude of growth of school spending is startling. Most reform proposals simply make no mention of expenditure, implicitly arguing that "getting the right programs" is all that matters. One explanation for the inattention to costs is that a widespread belief in the need for educational improvement has coincided with a pattern of decreased student enrollment, which in turn has allowed per-student expenditure to rise faster than total spending (and, presumably, than tax revenues and tax rates). But student populations are already rising again. This in turn may signal new problems for schools if taxpayers react by turning down requests for new funds.

Today most discussions of educational costs focus on the funding (or, more commonly, lack of funding) for specific new programs. The preceding analysis, however, demonstrates that schools have not been starved of funds. Perhaps reformers should really be asking not where new money for schools is to come from, but whether schools spend existing funds wisely.

The fact that educational expenditure has increased does not necessarily mean that it should not increase further. When the amounts various nations spend on schooling as a proportion of the gross domestic product (GDP) are compared, the United States ranks far from the top of the list, and some argue that this relative parsimony may help to explain the lagging performance of American students. We will argue, however, that significant changes in spending patterns will be required if student performance is to be enhanced by any additional funding. This argument flows naturally from findings that past spending increases have not been translated effectively into improved student performance.

The History of Performance Decline

Concerns about student performance are widespread. For two decades, the average high school students have had such mediocre

scores on the Scholastic Aptitude Test (SAT) that their performance has made front-page news. Local test results are also regularly reported in many metropolitan areas. The scores make
headlines usually because they are disappointing.

The basic facts make depressing reading:

—Student performance, as measured by a wide variety of
standardized tests, fell across the board during the 1970s.

—During the 1980s some measures of student performance
began to improve (from the depressed levels of the 1970s), but
others showed only maintenance of a dismal status quo.

—The average minority student consistently performs less
well than the typical white student, even though a modest narrowing of the gap has occurred during the past decade and a half.

—Students from the United States perform worse than those
from many other countries. Although some variation occurs across
tests, there is little evidence of significantly narrowing international
performance gaps.

Assembling a complete, detailed picture from scattered and
often uncertain data is fraught with inevitable problems, but the
brow-beating headlines do seem to have accurately captured the
general tenor of American educational performance. National SAT
scores fell from the mid-1960s through the end of the 1970s, as
shown in figure 3-4, before beginning to recover, but the recovery
has been neither consistent nor sufficient to return performance to
its previous highs. The average test-taker in 1979 (the trough) was
performing at the thirty-ninth percentile in math and thirty-third
percentile in reading of the test-takers in 1963 (the peak). Although the college admission tests (SAT and ACT, or American
College Testing score) showed some of the largest declines in test
scores, other tests also showed very significant falls.

Results from the National Assessment of Educational Progress (NAEP) are particularly significant because these are the only
tests that provide data for a sampling of students who are statisti-
cally representative of the overall student population. These tests
cover reading, mathematics, and science for a random selection of
students of given ages. Although there are some differences between different tests in the series, these data (which are summa-

Figure 3-4. Average SAT Scores, All Test Takers and by Race, 1967–93

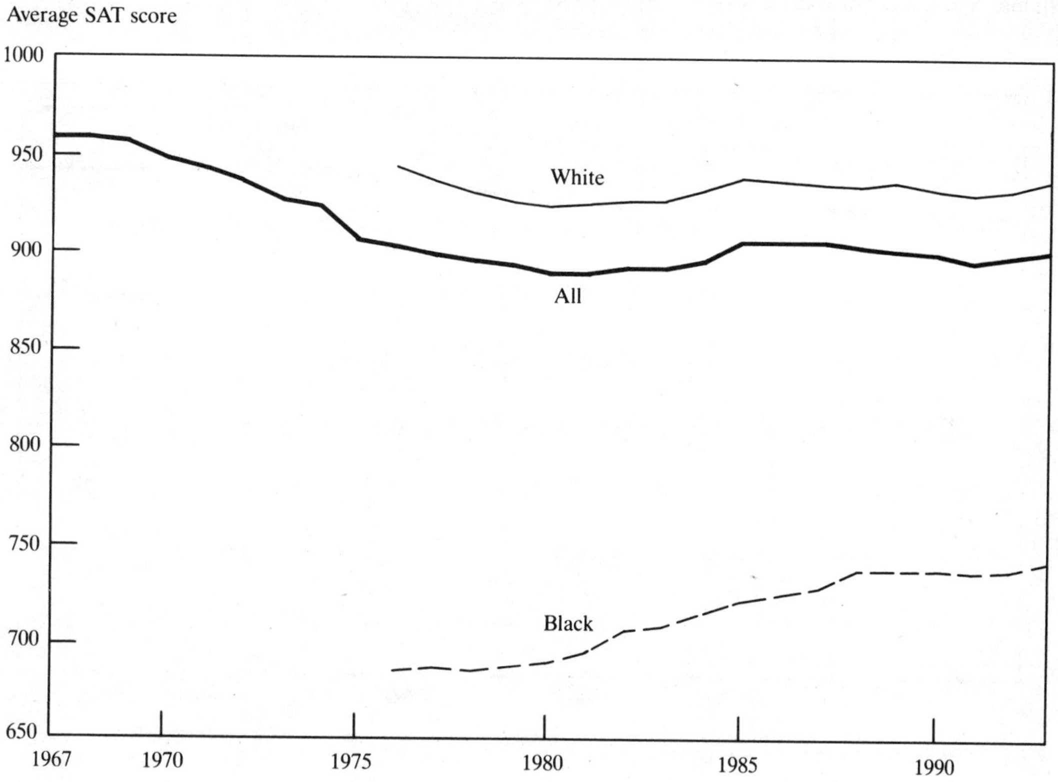

Average SAT score

SOURCE: U.S. Department of Education (1993).

rized in figures 3-5, 3-6, and S-2) suggest that the overall performance of the average seventeen-year-old student changed little between the early 1970s and 1990. Reading performance went up slightly, but mathematics performance showed no improvement, and science performance slipped. The performance gap between black and white students generally narrowed during this period, but it still remains unacceptably large.

International comparisons provide a different perspective on student performance. The most telling of the testing projects that have been undertaken during the past three decades is the International Assessment of Educational Progress (IAEP). The IAEP measures performance in science and mathematics, subjects less affected by possible language and cultural differences. It also uses

Figure 3-5. Reading Achievement of Seventeen-Year-Olds, by Race and Ethnicity, as Measured by the National Assessment of Educational Progress, 1971–92

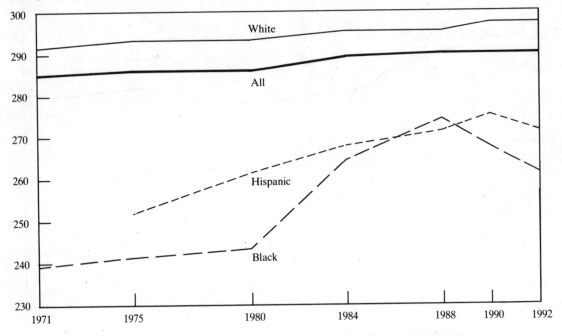

Average scale score

Source: U.S. Department of Education (1993).

the general tests developed for U.S. students, so any differences in curricular objectives or instructional approaches work in favor of U.S. students. Tables 3-3 and 3-4 show the performance of thirteen-year-olds from several countries and school systems on a battery of mathematics and science tests administered in 1989. American students are far from the top, and the gap is particularly large on more complex tasks. Moreover, as the report on the first IAEP mathematics results noted, the U.S. students seemed unworried by their performance: "Despite their poor overall performance, about two-thirds of the United States' thirteen-year-olds feel that they are 'good at mathematics.' Only 23 percent of their Korean counterparts, the best achievers, share the same attitude."

Figure 3-6. Mathematics Achievement of Seventeen-Year-Olds, by Race and Ethnicity, as Measured by the National Assessment of Educational Progress, 1973–92

Average scale score

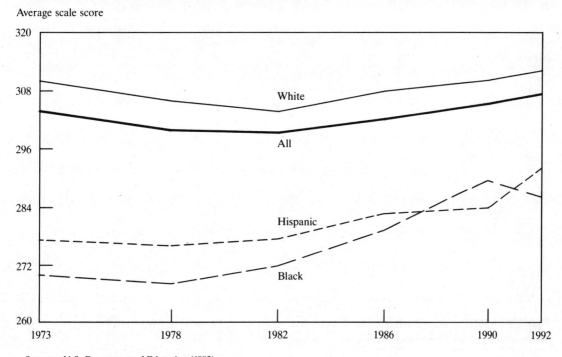

SOURCE: U.S. Department of Education (1993).

A smaller and different group of countries participated in a follow-up to the IAEP in 1991. On this collection of tests, nine-year-old students from the United States scored in the middle of the range on the science examination and at the bottom on the mathematics examination. Thirteen-year-old U.S. students scored at the bottom in both examinations.

Other tests confirm the IAEP's general findings. For example, the International Association for the Evaluation of Educational Achievement (IEA) compared international results on mathematics examinations given in both the mid-1960s and the early 1980s. These show American students generally falling behind students from both developed and developing countries.

43

Table 3-3. Comparative Performance of Thirteen-Year-Olds in Mathematics, as Measured by the International Assessment of Educational Progress, 1989

	Percentage performing at or above each level of competency (scale score)				
Country/region	*Add and subtract (300)*	*Simple problems (400)*	*Two-step problems (500)*	*Understand concepts (600)*	*Interpret data (700)*
Korea	100	95	78	40	5
Quebec (French)	100	97	73	22	2
British Columbia	100	95	69	24	2
Quebec (English)	100	97	67	20	1
New Brunswick (English)	100	95	65	18	1
Ontario (English)	99	92	58	16	1
New Brunswick (French)	100	95	58	12	<1
Spain	99	91	57	14	1
United Kingdom	98	87	55	18	2
Ireland	98	86	55	14	<1
Ontario (French)	99	85	40	7	0
United States	97	78	40	9	1

SOURCE: Lapointe, Mead, and Phillips (1989).

Table 3-4. Comparative Performance of Thirteen-Year-Olds in Science, as Measured by the International Assessment of Educational Progress, 1989

	Percentage performing at or above each level of competency (scale score)				
Country/region	*Know everyday facts (300)*	*Apply simple principles (400)*	*Analyze experiments (500)*	*Apply intermediate principles (600)*	*Integrate experimental evidence (700)*
British Columbia	100	95	72	31	4
Korea	100	93	73	33	2
United Kingdom	98	89	59	21	2
Quebec (English)	99	92	57	15	1
Ontario (English)	99	91	56	17	2
Quebec (French)	100	91	56	15	1
New Brunswick (English)	99	90	55	15	1
Spain	99	88	53	12	1
United States	96	78	42	12	1
Ireland	96	76	37	9	1
Ontario (French)	98	79	35	6	<1
New Brunswick (French)	98	78	35	7	<1

SOURCE: Lapointe, Mead, and Phillips (1989).

The one examination showing a somewhat different result is the 1991 Reading Literacy Study. Fourteen-year-old Americans placed seventh out of nineteen international testing groups. Unfortunately, no historical data exist on reading performance, so no conclusions about changes in performance can be drawn. Reading is also a very difficult subject to test and to compare internationally.

A related issue concerns the performance of the very top students. Many analyses of labor markets and the macroeconomy indicate that the very highly skilled—for example, scientists and engineers—play a particularly important role in determining the viability of the economy and its future growth. Thus, a fall in the performance of the highest performing students, particularly a disproportionate fall, might have especially adverse effects. Existing data and testing methodology make it difficult to ascertain with confidence whether the performance of top students has declined, as some measures have suggested. No evidence, however, indicates that their performance has improved.

Sources of Uncertainty about Performance

The paucity of any consistent and accepted national measures of student performance frustrates any detailed analysis. The SAT is the only examination to provide nationwide data on student performance over an extended period of time. Only those students who wish to go on to certain colleges or universities take that test, however. The possibility that the mix of students who take the SAT has changed over the years raises doubts as to whether average scores on this test reflect changes in the performance of the student population as a whole. The proportion of high school graduates taking the test held constant or fell throughout the 1970s but increased noticeably during the mid- to late 1980s. If increasing numbers of poorer prepared students take the test, changes in scores over time could result more from the composition of the test-taking population than from what students are learning. Similarly, the test itself can change over time, so that changes in the average scores may not fully reflect differences in performance. Extensive analysis of each of these possibilities, both for the SAT and for other tests, such as Iowa achievement tests, suggests that the tests do not reflect the performance of the whole population of students with unflagging accuracy. Nonetheless, these analyses do discern a general pattern of decline.

Nor are the data able to elucidate fully the composition of performance change. Specifically, some analyses have suggested that the character of performance has changed significantly. The decline in scores appears, by some tests, to have come more from higher-level skills than from basic, or lower-level, skills. The recovery may have come more from improvement in basic skills and less from higher-level skills. One cannot have full confidence in these generalizations, but they do suggest a greater decline in the most important dimensions of schools than the overall scores indicate.

Although the details of educational performance remain vague, the broad-brush conclusions are very consistent. Nobody would argue that student performance has improved during the past three decades. At best, it has remained relatively flat. At worst, it has fallen every bit as dramatically as the SAT scores indicate.

The Sources of Change in Performance

Schools are not solely responsible for the scholastic performance of their students. Parents and others outside of schools have a very large influence. This fact is not particularly surprising, given that students spend only five or six hours a day for 180 days out of the year in school, but it raises questions about how much schools can improve educational performance on their own.

Some aspects of family life and the socioeconomic environment surrounding schools have undoubtedly worsened in recent decades. The composition of families has changed dramatically, with more children living in single-parent families. The incidence of poverty among children, after falling in the 1970s, has risen to the levels of the early 1960s. Persistent welfare support has increased. Schools now compete for students' time and attention with video games, fifty or more television channels, and other attractions. Moreover, increased immigration has put new pressures on schools, especially in a handful of areas with large immigrant populations. These immigrants bring generally lower incomes, different languages, and a variety of cultural adjustment problems to the schools.

Not all changes have been for the worse. The adult population has higher levels of schooling than at any point in the past. Families are generally smaller, allowing for more attention to each child. And a variety of governmental programs—including expanded health care for the poor, food and nutrition programs, and preschool programs—have been developed to ameliorate the difficulties that disadvantaged families face.

Good or bad, none of these outside factors is a convincing explanation, either individually or jointly, for the uncomfortable fact that improvements in academic performance have not accompanied the tremendous increases in school spending. School districts commonly labeled "good"—districts with adequate resources, serving relatively advantaged student populations, and free of the pressures of immigrants—have had the same sorts of performance problems as the nation as a whole. Although such districts have generally increased spending at least as fast as the national average, they have been unable to convert more resources into higher performance.

Poor performance in education presents hard policy problems. Clearly, overall student performance would improve if more parents motivated their children to do better in school and if more parents took an active interest in their children's schooling. Direct comparisons of schools in the United States with those of Japan, for example, dramatically illustrate the effects of differences in parental attitudes. Parents in Japan demand, and support, higher academic achievement; American parents appear ambivalent about achievement. This lack of family support may, in fact, offer a severe constraint on the possibilities. At the same time, the policy options for changing parents' behaviors appear fairly limited, particularly in the short run. Exhorting parents to do a better job has not proved very effective, and nobody has yet articulated effective policies for developing more educationally active parents. Thus, for the most part, policymakers who want to improve student performance can concentrate only on schools.

Bibliographic Notes

Overall expenditure levels are found in various general data sources, including U.S. Bureau of the Census (1975), O'Neill and Sepielli (1985); Nelson (1991), Organization for Economic Co-operation and Development (1992, 1993), U.S. Department of Education (1993a), and Salganik and others (1993). State patterns are traced in Grymes and Harworth (1992). Medical expenditure comparisons rely on Newhouse (1992), where some of the issues of the proper deflator are discussed. The decomposition of costs along with the analysis of relative teacher earnings and special education is detailed in Hanushek and Rivkin (1994). The relative teacher earnings data come from the decennial censuses between 1940 and 1990. School demographic projections are based on the background paper by Lewis Solmon and Steven Rivkin. Changing family circumstances and their implications for schooling are developed by Moynihan (1986). See also Congressional Budget Office (1985). McDonnell and Hill (1993) analyze the responses of schools to influxes of immigrants. Discussions of special education and school funding can be found in Hartman (1980), Singer and Butler (1987), and Monk (1990). The cost estimates for special education rely on the review and analysis in Chaikind, Danielson, and Brauen (1993). See also Lankford and Wyckoff (1993), who provide detailed cost breakdowns for New York State. The view on administrative expenditure by then-Secretary of Education Bennett is found in Bennett (1988, p. 46).

The summary of school performance trends is based on the background paper by Eric Hanushek and Richard Sabot. Detailed data and evaluation comes from several important studies. A thorough review of trends in test scores and possible explanations of these is provided in Congressional Budget Office (1986, 1987), under the primary authorship of Daniel Koretz. Results on adult literacy are presented in Kirsch and others (1993). Discussions of SAT scores and trends in other tests include Wirtz and others (1977), Breland (1979), Behrendt, Eisenach, and Johnson (1986), Dynarski (1987), Crouse and Trusheim (1988), Koretz and others (1991), Bishop (1991), Hanushek and Taylor (1990), and U.S. Department of Education (1993a). International comparisons on IEA tests, IAEP tests, and other multicountry efforts can be found in Husén (1967), McNight and others (1987), Garden (1989), Lapointe, Mead, and Phillips (1989), Medrich and Griffith (1992), Stevenson and Stigler (1992), Shanker (1993), and Organization for Economic Co-operation and Development (1992, 1993). Detailed analysis of further NAEP results (history and literature) is developed in Ravitch and Finn (1987). Considerations of extremes of the distribution are found in Congressional Budget Office (1986) and Educational Testing Service (1991).

4

Economic Principles: A Guide for Improvement

Education's status quo is not sustainable. America will not, indeed cannot, continue to spend more and more on education to achieve flat or falling performance. The rapidly increasing costs of the educational system are already bumping against limited resources. Despite the nation's overall healthy economic growth, the living standards of America's middle class are, by some measures, stagnating. At the same time Americans are demanding that the government spend more on health care, social security, the environment, and other government programs. Legitimate public and private desires compete with schools for limited resources. One way or another, the United States must choose where to put its resources, and the nation's future well-being will depend on the wisdom of these choices. The question is how best to choose.

As economists, we believe that economic principles are a crucial part of any reasonable procedure for making decisions about the allocation of economic resources. At best such principles have been inconsistently applied in the education debate. Sometimes they have been completely ignored. We believe that the unhappy state of public education is largely the result of inattention to three decisionmaking principles designed to ensure that schools' resources are productively employed: efficient use of resources, implementation of appropriate performance incentives, and continuous learning from experience.

1. Efficient use of resources is paramount.

Perhaps the most fundamental economic principle is that resources should be used in the most efficient manner possible. In simplest terms, this means that any funds devoted to schools should be put to their best possible use. When a choice is made between two programs, put the funds into the program that achieves the best results for the money spent. If a program or activity does not contribute to students' performance, do not put funds into it. These precepts make so much common sense that resistance to them would seem impossible. But resistance there is.

Much of the resistance seems to come from a fundamental misunderstanding of the idea of efficiency as it is applied to education. Many people immediately assume that efficiency is either very narrow or very mechanical. Efficiency does not mean minimizing costs without regard to the results, nor does it mean creating a rigid structure for schools, in which only approved "efficient" educational techniques can be employed. What efficiency does mean is simply that costs and benefits should continually be compared and that costly programs with few benefits should be abandoned.

Although some argue that education is too important to be managed by concerns about costs and efficiency, we argue that education is too important not to be managed by those concerns. The United States must do everything possible to ensure that it reaps the largest possible educational gain from the resources available. So long as benefits exceed costs, decisionmaking based on efficiency calculations will ensure that funds are made available even for expensive projects. A productive educational project is more likely to go unfunded when efficiency is not considered, because narrow political considerations are then more likely to sway decisions.

Evidence, described in chapter 5, indicates clearly that schools often use their resources inefficiently. Inefficiency drains off funds and thwarts achieving superior performance for all students. To put it more positively, if schools were made more efficient, funds would be released for new and innovative programs that could help students improve their performance.

2. Appropriate performance incentives are the surest way to improve educational performance and to ensure the efficient use of resources.

Using resources efficiently is difficult, especially when the object of concern is something as complicated as education and schools. It is particularly difficult if the participants—the students, teachers, and principals—have limited interest in increased performance or the conservation of resources. This lack of interest characterizes the current schooling system. Improved academic performance is rarely rewarded, indeed, it is sometimes punished. Instead of rewarding good results, as the economist would favor, the current system concentrates much more on taking away individual initiative and incentives and replacing these with central direction.

Concentrating on performance incentives is the approach most likely to lead to improved schools. There are two basic approaches to decisionmaking in education: regulation and incentives. Regulation is a centralized command and control system based on punishment. Central management creates a system of rules; those under its control are punished if they do not obey. Incentives are a decentralized system based on rewards. Central management specifies a set of desired outcomes and rewards those school personnel (and students and parents) who achieve them. Typically incentives specify the goal and leave it to the agent to decide how to achieve it; regulatory regimes attempt to specify both the goal and the way it is to be reached.

Schools today rely far more heavily on regulation than on incentive. The appeal of regulation is that it allows central authorities at the state or school district level to control the processes and the activities of individual schools, ensuring that no locality or school strays too far from acceptable, general goals.

But regulation-based systems of management have drawbacks when used in education. Systems of regulations implicitly assume a single, well-defined, "best" way of educating. At best, regulatory systems ignore local differences, such as those arising from varying local objectives, differing student needs, or local initiatives in teaching approach. Worse, regulatory schemes can promote inefficiency by preventing local schools from adopting useful local variations. Regulatory systems are often costly and complicated to manage, because of the cost and difficulty of monitoring the actual performance of agents to ensure they are obeying the rules. So even when central decisionmakers seek desirable outcomes, they may be thwarted by an inability to determine who is behaving properly and who is not. Most important for education, regulations are likely to be too blunt and imprecise for use in a field that depends so much upon individual actions.

Education is a highly decentralized activity. Almost all productive work is done in individual classrooms. Creating a single set of regulations capable of identifying, hiring, and mobilizing almost three million teachers is next to impossible. The difficulties of applying strong regulatory regimes to education produce a persuasive argument for examining the case for management by incentives. Schools today make little use of performance incentives, and the results are all too evident.

Schools, like all other organizations, develop a series of implicit and explicit incentives for the people in them. People respond to incentives—be they financial, emotional, or some other form of reward. When rewarded for taking a specific action, people tend to take it. Students, teachers, and other school personnel respond just the same as other people. Unfortunately, few of the existing incentives within schools relate directly to student performance. As discussed later, few pay, promotion, or assignment decisions rest on a teacher's accomplishment in the classroom. Yet a variety of programmatic and classroom decisions have a direct bearing on teachers' workload and other school activities, regardless of their effect on student achievement. Poorly defined and often conflicting incentives simply do not push strongly for better outcomes in schools.

At the same time it is insufficient simply to direct schools to use performance incentives. The problem with applying performance incentives to the management of education is defining what sort of incentives will work most effectively without also having undesirable side effects. Nobody knows what incentives work effectively in the varied settings of the nation's schools. Several conceptually appealing incentive frameworks exist, as detailed in chapter 6. But, limited experience with direct performance incentives suggests that extensive experimentation will be required to determine which incentives will work best in the nation's schools.

3. Sustained improvement requires learning from experience.

Today's schools frequently adopt new programs and pursue altered activities in the name of improved performance. We too are calling for changes in school programs, albeit ones differing in focus from those commonly introduced. We want schools to adopt a stronger performance objective and to reflect the importance of high performance in much more explicit incentive structures. Both traditional school reforms and those proposed here have one thing in common: Their ultimate success depends crucially on the ability to identify and separate good change from bad. Schools must learn from their experiences.

Today, America's schools only teach. They themselves have little motivation to learn. Working and workable programs are difficult to find because schools all too often fail to monitor systematically the success or failure of programs now in place.

Today almost all formal evaluation of new educational schemes ceases before the plan actually goes into operation. One reason for this is a frequent lack of clarity, and sometimes actual disagreement, about the desired outcomes. Another reason is that many outcomes are hard to measure. And a final, more damning, reason is that few people in education have any reason to measure outcomes because few are rewarded on the basis of their ability to achieve specified outcomes.

Learning is hard. It requires more than a simple statement about what does and does not work; it requires a wealth of information to disentangle the key factors in the success or failure of any venture from the environment in which they succeeded or failed. Milwaukee, for example, now runs a voucher scheme that enables parents to choose the school—public or private—their children will attend. Because so few localities have experimented with voucher schemes, it is tempting to generalize from Milwaukee's experience to all voucher schemes. But it would be wrong to do so. The Milwaukee choice program is one specific and highly constrained use of vouchers, and it is embedded in a particular urban setting with an existing set of public and private schools. Disentangling the causes of any successes or failures of the Milwaukee program will be extraordinarily difficult; transferring such a program to other localities will necessarily be fraught with uncertainty.

And herein lies the real difficulty with the poverty of experimentation in education. Lack of learning breeds lack of learning. Schools not only lack good answers to the problems that beset them, but they are not generating answers that will help in the future. There is no systematic approach to learning from existing or proposed programs, so, although the Milwaukee choice program has had ongoing evaluation, there is little information from any other voucher program to compare with these results. In fact many of the most celebrated intervention programs in place today have no regular or systematic evaluation attached to them.

In the private sector productive and profitable enterprises are always learning. They are constantly modifying their approach and trying to better their performance. They have two advantages over schools. First, they generally find it easier to agree on performance measures and the definition of desirable outcomes. Standard information on profitability and return on investment gives immediate information on outcomes. Second, competition forces an external discipline. Those that do not learn, that do not adapt to changed conditions and improved technologies, find their profits slipping and may even cease to exist. But schools, faced with less clear direct measures of performance and seldom facing bankruptcy, have not felt the same pressure to learn from their own experiences and from the experiences of others.

For example, the Rochester, New York, City School District embarked in 1986 on a nationally acclaimed reform. The multi-million dollar restructuring included salary increases in excess of 40 percent for the typical teacher over the first three contract years, along with commitments to evaluate teacher performance. Although remnants of the plan—as well as its costs—remain today, the hoped-for change died in subsequent contract negotiations concerning performance evaluation. At no time from 1986 to the present has serious evaluation of the effectiveness of the plan been undertaken. And little has been learned from it.

Much is to be learned about the rewards and punishments that will promote improved student achievement in the various conditions with which America's schools must cope. Harnessing change and experimentation requires, as outlined in chapter 7, a plan for systematic evaluation or results. Such evaluation requires a clear delineation of what is to be produced along with suitable measures of that performance. Beyond that, however, achieving a high rate of progress demands a consistent strategy for trying out new approaches and for integrating the results of different experiences.

The fundamental point remains, however, that general school improvement is quite unlikely unless the future is built on a strong foundation of knowledge about what has and has not worked in the past. The culture of today's schools does not value learning from experience. Moreover, the states and the federal government provide limited guidance, resources, and direction in developing information about success and failure, even though these bodies are the logical centers of such learning. If the nation is to progress toward a better performing school system, experimentation and evaluation cannot be viewed as a pro forma but largely superfluous activity. It must be considered integral to the structure of change and improvement.

These decision rules for selecting what works and eliminating what does not do not remove the need for creative and competent leaders. They provide a framework for deciding on alternatives and for developing an improvement plan. They do not provide the plan. Nor do the rules substitute for teachers and school personnel of high quality. Quite to the contrary, we envision them as a way to ensure that those people control the schools.

These rules, concentrating on the efficient and effective use of resources, also do not eliminate the need for careful consideration of equitable outcomes. The United States is committed to equity, and its people and their political leaders have a continuing responsibility for ensuring that the schools fulfill the needs of disadvantaged and minority students. Those needs are easiest to meet when existing resources are employed as productively as possible.

Bibliographic Notes

A general discussion of variants of efficiency and benefit-cost analysis in education can be found in Levin (1976, 1983a, 1983b), Hanushek (1976), and Lockheed and Hanushek (1994). More general discussions of benefit-cost analysis are available in Gramlich (1990), Weimer and Vining (1992), and Zerbe and Dively (1994). An early discussion of misuses of efficiency ideas in schools is found in Callahan (1962); it traces the history of scientific management in schools and emphasizes the need for considering quality along with costs. An interim evaluation of Milwaukee's choice program is found in Witte, Bailey, and Thorn (1993). Marshall and Tucker (1992) provide a history of the Rochester reform efforts, which were based on Task Force on Teaching as a Profession (1986).

CHANGE

Economically Realistic Alternatives for Education in the Twenty-First Century

5

The Unperceived Range of Choices

Every school administrator, whether at the district or state level, has in a desk drawer a list of promising new school programs for which there is no funding. This does not make the schools uniquely underprivileged. In no field of human endeavor is there ever consistently as much money as there are good ideas to spend it on. But schools do seem to make things particularly hard on themselves. This chapter examines the way that decisions about programs have been made in schools, and it finds that school administrators stack the odds against change in a variety of ways. They make it hard to remove unsuccessful old programs, and they provide few incentives to introduce new ones. The result is an unsatisfying inertia, in which most reform activities are left either to await future funding or to be introduced only as small-scale demonstration experiments.

Inevitably, most discussions of reform take the base of current activities as their starting point. Equally inevitably, these current activities include programs that never proved productive. These programs typically have a constituency of supporters, made up of the personnel directly involved in them, the parents of specific students, and the program designers. So it is nearly always easier to win support for new programs that are added to the existing structure rather than offered as substitutes. Although this tactic may be understandable from the viewpoint of school administrators, it severely constrains schools' ability to improve.

Further constraints come from the lack of incentives for teachers and administrators to promote change. Although public statements about school reform concentrate on student achievement and performance, the plain fact is that rewards to any individual in the system are not very closely linked to student performance. If a group of students performs well, the relevant teachers and principal may gain considerable satisfaction. But they are unlikely to receive any substantial material reward for their efforts. It is also unlikely that unusually good results will noticeably affect their career paths. Careers of teachers and administrators are determined more by longevity and graduate schooling than by accomplishments with students.

Incentives for cost savings are even fewer. Schools offer virtually no rewards for those who do things more efficiently. There are some exceptions. For example, school districts often announce intentions to conserve on resources to limit the burden on taxpayers and thus to win support for school budgets, along with praise for school management. Yet, these calls are often overwhelmed by countervailing calls to increase expenditure to improve the quality of education. Announcements of "cutbacks" and "savings" by schools frequently amount to slower-than-projected or -desired growth in budgets, rather than true reductions in spending.

Much of the current discussion of school reform involves rather simplistic extensions of existing programs, often just doing more of the same. The vast majority of reform proposals have not looked at evidence about the success of similar policies at other schools. (Moreover, as we continually note, few schools attempt to evaluate success or failure, so the possibility for learning from others' experience is limited.)

In this chapter we return to the two simple tests, discussed in the previous chapter, to evaluate school programs. First, any proposal or policy that involves increased expenditures should ensure a commensurate increase in student performance. Second, proposals should be compared with each other, and the alternative that achieves the greater performance gains for any given expenditure should be chosen. Most recent reforms are likely to fail these tests.

Resource Usage

School programs are reformed at two levels: state and district. Changes in specific programs or curricular activities are typically proposed at the district level. For example, a district might propose a new program to coordinate efforts of a classroom aide and the school's remedial reading teacher to help students who have fallen more than one grade level behind the norm. Or it might propose to improve daily attendance patterns by equipping an attendance officer with modern computer and telephone technology. Or it might suggest integrating computers into mathematics instruction to relieve teachers of the work of conducting drills and monitoring progress. These programs are detailed plans for using school resources. Each of these suggestions requires expansions to the current budget. They are also quite marginal. They may add to existing programs, but they typically do not question what exists. Thus most programs and activities, accounting for the bulk of expenditure and administration and teaching effort, remain outside the scope of district-level policy discussions.

General issues of resource allocation are typically addressed at the state level, where decisions are made about commitments to improve the overall school system, including increasing overall spending, reducing class sizes, raising the starting or average level of teacher salaries, and adding new requirements for advanced teaching degrees or specific kinds of teacher preparation.

Somewhere between the two levels of the school debate, crucial questions get lost. Existing programs and resource usage are not questioned, nor are trade-offs between programs examined. Instead reform becomes enrichment. The only way to change schools is to add to existing programs, in part because that is the only thing the administrative process as now structured seems to be able to do.

To distinguish between effective and ineffective programs, schools must be able to measure their results. Many views on the efficacy of a school's activities or approaches are currently shaped by casual observation and anecdotal evidence—after all, every parent and educator has gone through school. Unfortunately, such observations can be very misleading. To make judgment harder still, schools are just one factor in a student's achievement—alongside the student's own drive and ability and the influence of parents, friends, and others. The task of research into school performance is to separate the influences of the various factors to discover just what schools do and do not do. Not all research into education is equally suited for this task, and in this report we have paid particular attention to results using appropriate methodology for the specific task of separating the effects of school resources from the effects of other influences on student performance. Econometric techniques, a sophisticated form of statistical analysis, have been used extensively during the past quarter century to do just this. The results of these analyses create our deep skepticism about the overall course of basic school policy.

Although some efforts have been made to look at specific programs, the most compelling evidence on school performance comes from direct investigation of the effects of key identifiable resources devoted to teaching and instruction. These investigations examine actual decisions about resources made by administrators and teachers operating within schools as they are organized today. Contrary to conventional wisdom, little systematic relationship has been found between school resources and student performance. Any findings showing that increases in basic school resources promote higher achievement are balanced by those showing the opposite.

The research findings translate directly into observations about individual school systems. Some public schools appear to use money and other resources effectively, but others do not. In fact, resources are spent so ineffectively so often that we would expect no overall improvement in student performance from increased resources.

Such a statement, with its obvious ramifications for educational policy, needs both documentation and further discussion to ensure that it be correctly understood. It is not a statement of inevitability. Nor is it a statement about every school system. It is, however, a statement about what we currently observe, given the institutional structure and incentives that exist. At the very least, the results suggest overwhelmingly that school administrators are not monitoring the performance of their programs or the effectiveness of resource usage. More important, a quick survey of policies and programs with little or no detectable benefits lists many of the same ones for which school reformers have campaigned most vigorously—and still do.

Take class size. The intuitively appealing idea that smaller classes will improve student learning is a perennial cornerstone of educational reform. But it is an idea that is not supported by evidence. Because reduced class size is so popular as a policy instrument, its effectiveness is perhaps the most researched topic in education. The previously discussed econometric evidence shows vividly that across-the-board reductions in class size are unlikely to yield discernible gains in overall student achievement. Moreover, this empirical evidence on the limited relationship between class size and student performance is supported by direct experimental evidence, most recently from an extensive experiment by the State of Tennessee (see box 7-4). Yet, as documented in chapter 3, much effort and money has been expended during the past half century to encourage broad-scale reductions in class sizes and pupil-teacher ratios.

The evidence does not say that small classes are never useful. Specific situations may lend themselves to smaller classes, just as other situations may lend themselves to larger classes. For example, the description of experiences in individual tutorial programs emphasizes the potential achievement gains from intensive programs for poorly performing students (box 5-1). A tutorial program developed at the University of Texas at Dallas has also shown that remedial programs can be cost-effective. But this evidence does not imply a need for across-the-board reductions in class sizes. Specialized intervention programs may help low-achieving students, but the available evidence suggests that higher-achieving students can be placed in larger classes without jeopardizing their achievement—thus holding overall costs constant. Indeed, in Japan teachers and administrators expressly trade large class sizes for more time for teacher preparation (box 5-2). Overall decreases in class size have often been set by general school board policy or

Box 5-1. One-to-One Tutoring

Robert Slavin and his colleagues at Johns Hopkins have developed and successfully deployed in inner-city schools an intensive early education program to bring all children to grade level in reading by the third grade. "Success for All" is a resource-intensive approach, which includes several interrelated interventions—high-quality preschool and kindergarten programs for all children, one-on-one tutoring for low-achieving students, research-based reading methods in all grades, frequent assessments of reading progress, and family support programs. The plan was first implemented during the 1987–88 school year at Abbottston Elementary School in Baltimore, an inner-city school of approximately 440 students. By the spring of 1993, Success for All had been introduced in thirty-one schools in twelve states.

Tutors are certified teachers who work individually with students who have difficulty reading. In twenty-minute sessions, tutors use different strategies from those used in regular reading classes to teach the same skills. Student progress is assessed at least once every eight weeks. Moreover, a family support team works in each school to encourage parents to support their children's efforts.

To evaluate the program, students in the five Success for All schools in Baltimore were matched and compared with students in similar neighboring schools. After three years in the program (four years for Abbottston), students in most of the schools showed substantial positive effects on most individually administered measures of reading. (Earlier testing with the California Achievement Tests [CAT] was apparently not repeated in the later evaluations, even though the early CAT results gave a different picture of the performance gains). Furthermore, the number of students who did

specific contract negotiation. Decreases are also included, albeit implicitly, with the introduction of many specific programs.

The cost implications of reductions in class sizes are significant. For example, dropping a class from twenty-five to twenty-two students increases classroom expenditures by more than 10 percent. But the evidence suggests that many teachers either do not react to such decreases or do not change what goes on in the classroom to capitalize effectively on the smaller class. Nonetheless, such marginal changes, applied over and over again, accounted for almost 30 percent of the increase in instructional staff expenditure during the last hundred years and for a much larger portion of the increase during the last two decades.

Another example of expensive, but empirically unjustified, policy reform is advanced degrees for teachers. States frequently require teachers to obtain advanced degrees as part of their normal

not advance to the next grade fell substantially, and all five schools showed improved attendance rates.

Success for All has demonstrated that early, immediate, and intensive intervention can noticeably improve student performance. Cost is a problem, however; the tutoring relies on certified teachers, making the program more expensive than typical federally funded programs for disadvantaged students.

A variant of one-to-one tutoring, instituted in Dallas, Texas, by George Farkas and his colleagues at the University of Texas at Dallas, substitutes hourly paid tutors at a considerable cost saving. This program does not involve major restructuring of the school and is limited to tutorial sessions with selected students. The direct instruction in the Structured Tutoring Program is, however, estimated to cost less than 40 percent of the typical amount spent on the federal compensatory education program in Dallas and a fourth of the Success for All program. Although comparative performance data are limited, initial estimates of performance gains appear similar to those of Success for All. The Texas program was introduced into twenty-six Dallas elementary schools in less than two years. Part of this expansion is driven by a new emphasis on student performance that has led individual principals to seek out more effective instructional methods.

These tutorial programs appear to have improved performance of disadvantaged students, a population that has proved to be exceedingly difficult to bring up to grade levels. Little is known, however, about how well these programs can be replicated elsewhere, about what structures are the most cost-effective, and about how these programs are best linked to the local curricula, teachers, and decisionmaking.

Sources: Madden and others (1993); Slavin and others (1990); and Farkas (1993a, 1993b).

certification process. Virtually every teacher in the country is presented with financial incentives to obtain graduate school credit. Salaries are routinely linked to graduate work. Yet once more conventional wisdom fails. Studies of student performance indicate no systematic difference between the average teacher with an advanced degree and the average teacher without one.

The evidence again does not indicate that advanced degrees never pay off in terms of higher student achievement. Some graduate programs are surely very skillful at improving a teacher's ability to manage classrooms and to engage students in learning. But the average graduate program, the one that is attended by the average teacher, does not noticeably enhance the teacher's ability to boost student achievement. Although they do not improve student performance, these programs are expensive both for the teachers who pay for them and for school systems that subse-

Box 5-2. Japanese Classrooms

Much recent attention has been devoted to Japanese schools and the lessons that can be learned from them. Part of this interest stems directly from the Japanese success in international markets, especially with electronics, automobiles, and other technologically sophisticated products where the quality of the labor force is a key ingredient. Another part comes from head-to-head comparisons of academic performance. For example, in the Second International Mathematics Study conducted in 1980–82, 58 percent of Japanese students at the completion of high school were rated as "high performance students," while only 3 percent of U.S. students achieved that rating. Only 5 percent of U.S. students performed above the median for Japanese students.

Japanese and U.S. schooling systems, family attitudes, and culture differ dramatically. In their in-depth study of U.S. and Asian schools, Harold Stevenson and James Stigler documented several fundamental differences, many of which range far beyond school policy. Japanese families appear much more committed to the schooling of their children than U.S. families do; the Japanese society as a whole is much more homogeneous in culture, attitudes, and beliefs; the educational system is very highly centralized; and teachers have very high status.

These extensive differences between the two school systems clearly make it inappropriate to attribute performance differences to any specific aspect of schools or families. Similarly, adapting any single part of the Japanese system in U.S. schools will not

quently pay higher salaries to reflect the training. More perversely, because teachers are not necessarily looking for any specific skills but are simply satisfying the degree requirements, graduate schools are faced with incentives to water down the curriculum. The quality of the graduate program seldom has any bearing on pay or promotion opportunities within any system.

Teachers are also rewarded for experience in the classroom, although there is little convincing evidence concerning the effectiveness of this qualification. Some research suggests significant performance gains by teachers, particularly from the first few years of experience. The bulk of the evidence, however, is inconclusive, with several other studies showing a falloff in student performance with higher levels of teacher experience—perhaps reflecting a gradual loss of the teacher's enthusiasm and energy.

These specific factors—class size, teacher education, and teacher experience levels—are particularly frequent targets of policy change, aspects of schooling that would be improved if only

necessarily narrow the achievement gaps with Japan.

Nonetheless, various Japanese approaches to school organization do seem likely candidates for experimentation by some American state systems. Classroom organization is one straightforward example. Although the overall teacher-pupil ratio is similar in the two countries, the typical Japanese class is large, perhaps double the size of the typical U.S. class. Instead of spending most time in the classroom, as U.S. teachers do, Japanese teachers spend much more time preparing lessons (often with other teachers), working with individual students, evaluating and correcting homework, and the like. The larger Japanese classes allow the allocation of time by teachers and the organization of the classroom to be very different.

The obvious lesson for U.S. schools is that the possibilities for effective school organization are greater than many Americans now appreciate. In some cases, larger classes in some subjects may free resources for other, more valuable activities—for example, teacher preparation or specialized classes that can take better advantage of low student-teacher ratios. The Japanese experience illustrates that different organizations of classrooms and teaching can, in the right circumstances, yield high performance at resource costs similar to those in the United States.

Sources: Garden (1989); National Research Council (1993); Stevenson and Stigler (1992).

more resources were available. The data in fact clearly indicate that these are the very resource uses that have been broadly instituted in the postwar period. Class sizes have fallen, the proportion of teachers with master's degrees has risen, and teachers have increasing amounts of teaching experience. Each of these requires added resources. Costs have risen, but student performance has not.

Class size, teacher education, and teacher experience levels are far from the only elements of conventional educational reform that miss the mark. Consider the frequent calls for either a lengthened school day or a lengthened school year. Such policy changes appeal to another commonsense notion—with more time, students would learn more. That notion is reinforced by hopes that American students would fare better in competition with students from other countries, such as Japan, if they spent a similar amount of time in school. Japanese students do indeed spend considerably more time in school each year, 220 days compared with 180 days in the United States, but there are many reasons to believe that the length of the Japanese school year alone is not the primary reason that Japanese students outperform U.S. students on standardized tests.

Little research has actually been conducted on the effects on performance of additional time spent in schooling. But with so much evidence already suggesting that existing instructional time could be used more effectively, proposals to add more ineffective instruction are highly questionable. Cost considerations reinforce this conclusion. Costs would be roughly proportional to increased time spent on schooling. A lengthening of school time by 20 percent, a figure frequently discussed, would lead to expenditure approximately 20 percent greater. It seems unlikely that many people would want to use this much additional funding simply to extend the school year when it could be used in a variety of other programs. Added resources and time could allow introduction of specific new programs, so it is not necessarily a matter of choosing expansion of the school year over other things. Nevertheless, pointing to presumed gains from simply expanding the current school year is an insufficient justification without explicit consideration of costs and alternative uses of resources.

Another popular policy proposal is to improve school leadership. Specifically, many people call for increasing the quality and authority of the school leadership, usually the principal. This argument comes from research that shows that effective schools frequently have particularly effective leadership. An effective leader may set high standards, getting teachers to work together and to perform at high levels. Alternatively or additionally, an effective principal may be able to put together a particularly competent team of teachers.

Although few would question the importance of effective leadership, the potential gains from pursuing such policies within the current structure of schools are uncertain. Just because some noticeably effective school leaders exist does not mean that schools know how to train or select such people on a broad scale. The current selection and preparation process for principals does not ensure that they are exceptional leaders. Moreover, the current rules, regulations, contracts, and operating principles of schools severely restrict what an individual principal can do. For example, few principals can make unilateral hiring and firing decisions about teachers. A principal may have a significant effect on the teachers in a specific school, but that will not necessarily improve schools in general. An effective principal may force a specific teacher to seek a different school, for example, but this will probably simply involve a reshuffling of teachers, so that the overall stock of teachers remains relatively unchanged. Therefore, if calls for improved leadership are to be effective, substantial (and usually unstated) changes must occur in the overall organization of the schools. (Calls for effective leadership also implicitly take the unlikely view that any changes will be costless.)

Educational research has also delved into a wide variety of specific programs, approaches to teaching, and the like. Some appear effective, others not. But little in the way of potential programs or policies appears reproducible across a wide range of circumstances. Programs that yield favorable results in one circumstance do not tend to show the same positive effects in other circumstances. The simple explanation is that the educational process is extraordinarily complex, making it impossible for researchers and policymakers alike to describe with sufficient accuracy the key elements of a program that could be successfully transported to new and different situations.

Two conclusions can, and should, be drawn from the evidence presented. First, a simple expansion of existing educational programs is unlikely to improve student achievement. Second, large amounts of resources currently are being used inefficiently, and these could be freed for more effective use. The evidence indicates that no single, clearly identifiable method can enhance student performance. Yet schools now focus much of their self-improving energies on finding just such a panacea, which, they seem to assume, will appear in the form of an enrichment of existing programs. Existing research all suggests a very different focus for policy.

Decisions, Resources, and Performance

Today's spending policies—the result of complex interactions among schools, school boards, parents, regulatory agencies, and government programs— fail at a variety of levels for a variety of reasons. Policies centrally directed by state and federal authorities cannot mandate in sufficient detail how resources should be employed to produce significant improvements in performance. Indeed, no single program, applied uniformly, appears capable of achieving uniform improvement. Local school boards and unions also contribute to the potential for inefficiency—and in some cases even appear to mandate it. Maximum class sizes and other negotiated work rules in contracts, for example, are undeniable improvements in the working environment for teachers, but they are expensive and are not directly related to student performance.

Reformers frequently argue that schools do not have to continue the ineffective use of resources. One common argument begins with the obviously true statement that past poor decisions need not imply future poor decisions. Some schools seem to use resources effectively. So surely there must be some way for all to use resources effectively. But the conclusion of this argument—"if we avoid bad uses of resources and direct funds well, added resources can make a real difference"—begs the question of how to use resources well in the first place. How do we identify what the good schools are doing right and apply those lessons to others?

Reformers also frequently point to the good results from a specific program, teaching approach, or organizational idea and then speculate about how added resources would permit the program to be instituted universally, thus creating universal improvement. Yet, on closer examination, the proposed programs have invariably had very limited application and have not been introduced in a majority of schools even within the districts that are identified as demonstrating the success of the particular intervention. Why, if these programs are so clearly effective, are they not adopted more readily in the very districts where information about them should be readily available?

Both of these arguments for added spending ignore the history of educational decisionmaking and spending. Central decisionmakers in Washington and in the state capitals have for years tried to specify how schools should use resources effectively. Local school boards have also developed plans for improving student performance through more effective operations. Yet neither has achieved results. The obvious—and obviously unanswerable—question for the proponents of further increases in spending is: why should the people currently making decisions do noticeably better with more money today when they have repeatedly failed to do better with more money in the past? Such an examination of history does not provide much optimism for reform as typically promoted. Moreover, because most of the requests for increased funding do not address the question of alternative ways of making decisions, the prospects for fundamental change are very limited.

Disadvantaged Students and Distributional Issues

Many have observed that students in high-spending districts in affluent suburbs consistently perform well on standardized tests and that more of these students go on to advanced education than do students from less affluent school districts. Comparing these results with the generally lower scores in inner cities—commonly perceived to be financially strapped—and in rural areas quite naturally suggests to many that resources are the issue. Unfortunately, the problems are not that simple. In fact, inner-city schools are frequently among the highest-spending schools in each state. The bulk of federal funding goes for categorical programs that benefit disadvantaged students, and many state-financed systems send disproportionate funds to inner-city schools through both general and categorical grant programs.

Second, and more important, the effect of schools on student performance must be separated from the effects of families and other factors. Families with higher incomes tend to be more educated, smaller, and more likely to have both parents present.

Raised with a greater emphasis on education and more encouragement to achieve, children from such families tend to be better prepared for school and to achieve at a higher level. Just the opposite holds for children from poorer families. Such differences hide the true impacts of their schools. Some effective schools remain unnoticed because they cannot overcome all the adverse conditions that lower their students' performance. Indeed, some teachers in schools classified as substandard dependably and regularly improve the performance of their students far more than the average teacher, yet they often cannot raise the absolute level of student performance above average. Similarly, ineffective teachers in affluent districts might achieve above-average performance from their students, even though the school is not providing a high-quality education. Therefore, simple observations about levels of performance provide little information about what the school is adding and may even be quite misleading. These factors obviously influence the effectiveness of school spending, and they also have direct policy implications.

Three conclusions come from these distributional considerations. First, low scholastic performance by disadvantaged students is a very serious problem that must be addressed. Second, performance problems by otherwise advantaged students cannot be ignored either; simply having students with above-average performance does not mean that the schools are doing a good job. Third, although society must seek solutions to both of these problems, the answer is not simply to provide more resources within the current structure.

Specifically, the problems of educating children from poor families, from racial and ethnic minorities, and from rural families are no more likely to be cured by simple expenditure policies than are the general problems of the whole system, even though a properly running system for the disadvantaged may require added expenditures. Programs to compensate for disadvantages of students suffer from the same problems that afflict the larger system: quality and effectiveness vary greatly, and few incentives for improvement are offered. Although central-city schools spend more than the average per pupil, is it enough? It is impossible to say, given current management. Simply increasing spending in schools serving disadvantaged populations is a poor solution to the societal problems revolving around low educational performance.

Some evidence suggests that expansion of early childhood programs may help, particularly for the disadvantaged. The problems of poor preparation and motivation in the home are magnified when students cannot keep pace in the classroom. Programs to provide greater resources in the prekindergarten years, especially if linked to school programs that capitalize on such investments, may be generally worthwhile, as described in box 5-3. Nevertheless, the evidence is equally clear that such investments will not by themselves equalize the educational performance of all groups in society. Moreover, these programs have also suffered from weak incentives to improve their effectiveness, to integrate them into traditional schooling, and to conserve on costs. So, although such programs show promise, they would be most effective if they were incorporated into the improved management and incentive structures discussed in the next chapter.

Computers, Television, and Other Technologies

Although easily taken for granted, the constancy of the organization and structure of the classroom—students gathered around a teacher—is in fact quite surprising, given the dramatic technological advances that have been made in recent decades. Computers, multimedia devices, expanded databases, and networks would seem to hold out so much promise for transforming the way children are taught; indeed, education can be thought of as a key part of the information industry. Several analyses have suggested real advantages to using certain kinds of technology for instructional purposes—including drill and practice activities on computers, some self-paced instruction, and use of radio or television for transmitting good teaching to distant locations. Yet even with the dramatic declines in their costs, computers and other electronic devices remain outside the mainstream of much of the instruction in U.S. schools. Computers, for example, are readily available in

Box 5-3. Early Childhood Education

Disadvantaged students enter school less prepared than more advantaged students, and this deficit has lasting effects. This observation has focused attention on preschool programs, the federal Head Start program in particular. Supporters of an expansion of Head Start note that the nearly thirty-year-old program has never been fully funded and urge that it be made an entitlement to low-income children. Detractors point out that evaluations of this program have not led to much optimism about its efficacy. The evidence shows that Head Start leads to immediate IQ gains but that these gains quickly disappear as the student goes through regular public schools.

The Perry Preschool Program, a program with a randomized experimental design, provides much of the available evidence on preschool education. Studies, with results beginning in 1982, followed students born between 1958 and 1962 from preschool until age nineteen. Students were tested at various ages, and their work and other experiences were analyzed. The students, who were randomly given an intensive preschool program (beyond most Head Start programs), had significantly better cognitive achievement, higher wages, better employment records, lower crime rates, among other desirable outcomes, than those in control groups who did not attend preschool. A recently published follow-up study, which extended the observations to age twenty-seven, suggests strong gains in wages and employment for the students receiving the preschool program. Moreover, an early cost-benefit analysis indicates that the expense of the preschool program may well be justified by the subsequent benefits to the participants.

The results from the Perry Preschool Program have been used by some to support an expanded Head Start program, but others still question the evidence. The Perry program evaluation involved only 123 chil-

many school systems, but they are seldom well integrated into the curriculum and instructional program.

Frequent and vehement predictions of movement toward new, more capital-intensive teaching technologies have never materialized. What the predictions seem to have missed is how the existing system of incentives in the schools would need to be altered to give new technologies a fair hearing.

Technology has not made more inroads into schools because it upsets the structure of personnel use and spending. Although dazzling multimedia displays might suggest otherwise, the clearest advantage of technological aids to instruction has been permitting equal outcomes at less cost than traditional instructional methods. They do not necessarily improve upon student performance, but they do save on resources by reducing the demand for school

dren, 58 of whom received the preschool treatment and 65 who did not. Its results appear completely at odds with much larger and more extensive evaluations of preschool programs.

Yet Steven Barnett, one of the authors of the original Perry evaluation, recently argued that the conflicts between the Perry study and the others may in fact be smaller than they at first seem. Although students who attended preschool generally did not score higher than their peers on IQ tests and other tests of cognitive achievement, these tests, he argues, are poor measures of more important outcomes such as wages and behavior. The studies show greater consistency when longer-term effects (third grade or later) are examined. The studies indicate that students with preschool tend to perform better in school, continue in school longer, and are placed in special education classes less often than similar students without preschool. Finally, some differences among studies may be explained by technical evaluation problems, such as the failure to test students who were held back a grade.

Taken together, the studies suggest that preschool programs may be good investments to improve the education of disadvantaged students. Nevertheless, the evidence is also remarkably thin, especially when the level of spending on these programs is considered. Federal funding of the Head Start program alone exceeded $3 billion in the 1994 fiscal year. The programs and evaluations that are cited to support large increases in this spending involve expenditures only in the range of hundreds of thousand dollars. The high costs and potential benefits of preschool programs make investments in more information about the effectiveness of preschool an unquestionably good idea.

Sources: Berrueta-Clement and others (1984); Gramlich (1986); Barnett (1992); Schweinhart, Barnes, and Weikart (1993); and U.S. Department of Education (1993b).

personnel. Moreover, the introduction of new technology often involves considerable start-up costs. These costs include initial capital expenditures, training of personnel, and development of appropriate curricular materials.

Such expenditures might save money in the long run, but rewards for saving money are not built into school systems. Therefore, it is not particularly surprising that little energy is devoted to selecting and installing new technologies that primarily involve substituting capital for labor—especially if these substitutions merely maintain existing levels of student performance. The exclusion of new technologies has meant that education remains an extremely labor-intensive industry, impervious to productivity improvements. Indeed, schools have gone in the opposite direction, demanding even more labor as they have reduced teacher-pupil ratios. The advantages that might come from improved educational technology, in particular from the substitution of capital for labor in schools, will not be fully realized as long as the incentives in schools remain unchanged.

Teachers are key to much of this discussion. When they are treated simply as employees of the schools and not as important decisionmakers in the educational process, they tend to revert to defensive positions, worrying about overall employment and working conditions. Without strong incentives to do so, they are unlikely to advocate the adoption of technologies that will require them as individuals to undertake increased training costs, and threaten them as a group with decreased employment possibilities—and in the next chapter we propose what some such incentives might be.

The Special Case of Teachers

Although there are great differences in performance among schools, there are even greater differences in quality among teachers. The specific teachers that a student has can make a tremendous difference in achievement. A series of good teachers can catapult a student ahead of others regardless of family background. Likewise, a series of bad teachers can stunt the development of a student, who, if unlucky enough to come from a poor family background, may never be able to recover. Research confirms what most parents observe: enormous differences in teaching abilities exist in virtually every school. Unfortunately, the standard ways to identify good teachers are quite unreliable. Graduate training, for example, is not a reasonable indicator of a good teacher. Worse, salary schedules generally do not link pay to teacher quality.

What can be done? Two general strategies have been employed to increase the numbers of good teachers, and these are frequently viewed as the only options available: mandatory qualifications for teachers and higher salary levels. Both policies, while recognizing the value of quality teachers, have nonetheless proved to be generally ineffective.

Teacher Certification

Regulated qualifications contained in state teacher certification rules require specific academic preparation and job experience and often involve tests of one sort or another. All are designed to define what makes for a good teacher and to ensure that schools select appropriately. Training, preparation, and certification requirements may have screened out some people who would be inappropriate for the classroom, but these devices are too crude and error prone to select consistently high-quality individuals. The extensive research into teaching performance has shown that the standard criteria for predicting the quality of teachers are not closely related to actual performance in the classroom. Therefore, refining this list of requirements is unlikely to be a productive way to proceed.

One key problem in predicting teacher quality is that managers using the criteria demand quantitative measurements, while the factors that actually relate to classroom performance are typically qualitative and vague. Even if the factors important in producing a good teacher were known, specifying true quality and implementation standards would still be exceedingly difficult. In the process of writing the certification regulations, which become enforceable legal documents, the essence of what is effective and how to identify it tends to get lost. For example, the number of semester hours of courses in pedagogy required to teach at a certain level can be specified, but neither the quality of the courses nor the behavioral outcomes of prospective teachers can be guaranteed. Moreover, the standards that are applied are generally based not on any empirical analysis, but on conceptual formulations about what somebody thinks is likely to be important or on the views of the institutions that prepare the teachers.

A particularly insidious problem with teacher certification is that it is frequently viewed as costless. Because no specific budgetary outlays are required, there is a tendency to presume that such regulations do not directly affect spending. But certification is not costless. Increasing the number of requirements prospective teachers must meet has been shown to reduce the supply of applicants and potential teachers, while guaranteeing little in the way of effectiveness. Many college students, it appears, are dissuaded from considering teaching because of the course and training requirements that states place on entry into teaching. In other words, obtaining teachers of any given quality is more expensive because of the regulations. Although the added expense might be worthwhile if the regulations were able to identify truly good teachers and ensure that every teacher entering the classroom was of high quality, the cost is hard to justify when the regulations fail to serve that purpose.

Teacher Salaries

The second policy aimed at improving the quality of teachers involves lifting the overall salary schedule. The idea behind higher salaries is to attract more, and more able, college students into teaching. The snag, however, is that the approach lifts everybody's salary, regardless of skills and abilities. Higher salaries will attract people who otherwise would have prepared for different jobs, but they will not distinguish between potentially good teachers and potentially bad ones. Whether higher salaries result in more capable teachers depends, among other things, on the quality of the hiring process of schools. It appears from existing evidence, however, that the average school system has a limited ability to predict who will be an effective teacher on the basis of information available before an individual has actually taught in the classroom.

Further, current evidence provides little indication that schools can transform poor teachers into good ones. Many schools, sometimes with state-level regulation or support, have adopted programs of in-service training and mentoring to improve teacher performance, but these programs have not proved to be very effective, particularly with exceptionally inadequate teachers. Although experience and practice contribute to better teaching performance, formal training seems to do little.

For the most part, schools now rely on teachers to manage their own careers. Beyond initial hiring, schools usually actively select teachers only when overall numbers are being reduced. (Even then, contract restrictions frequently specify exactly which teachers are to be eliminated, using decision rules that are unrelated to actual teacher performance). Otherwise the only adjustment in the teaching staff occurs when a teacher voluntary departs or retires. This current hiring structure has two shortcomings. First, schools have few mechanisms to dissuade a good teacher from leaving once that person is attracted to a different opportunity. Second, the options for dealing with teachers who are not performing well are extremely limited. Firing a teacher is not usually an option, even if mentoring or further training proves unsuccessful.

Under current school management, simply increasing teacher salaries, without changing hiring and retention policies, is wasteful and unappealing. Indeed, blanket statements about teacher salaries being either too high or too low do not have much meaning. Good teachers are absolutely essential to the high performance of schools, but policies that raise salaries while failing to recognize differences in the quality of teachers are very undesirable. Schools end up paying too much for low-quality teachers and too little for high-quality teachers.

Insisting on overall salary increases also prevents schools from attracting people with specific skills, such as math and science, that are highly valued in jobs competing with teaching. Remedying a shortage of teachers with particular skills by calling for overall increases in salaries regardless of skills dissipates available funds. To use available funds effectively, teacher salaries must reflect the ease or difficulty of attracting and retaining teachers with particular skills, such as those with math or science specialties. Various arguments about equity among teachers notwithstanding, overall salary increases create significant added expense.

Evidence and Policy

Strong evidence shows that continuing the policies of the past is extraordinarily expensive and unproductive. Expanding upon them would be worse. Even disregarding costs, neither across-the-board regulatory changes nor general spending increases within the current structure are likely to improve the schools.

Abandoning these past policies would open up a broad range of options. Specifically, reversing wasteful policies can free up resources that can be applied elsewhere. For example, individual schools may find that trading off some large classes for small, specific-purpose classes is sensible (even though it may not be possible under current regulations and contracts). Similarly, a school may wish to employ a local engineer at a high but part-time salary to teach an advanced science course. Or, it may wish to follow the Japanese model and have generally larger classes. The options are more numerous than many might think.

Bibliographic Notes

The investigation of the effectiveness of school resources is commonly traced to the "Coleman Report" (Coleman and others, 1966). The early controversy caused by these findings can be seen in Mosteller and Moynihan (1972). The general discussions of current evidence about relationships between school resources and performance are drawn from reviews of the econometric literature in Hanushek (1986, 1989). These reviews summarize and evaluate existing econometric studies through 1989 of input-output relationships in education. More recent studies of that genre are consistent with the earlier studies. Consideration of the underlying statistical issues and the policy interpretation of these results is found in Hedges, Laine, and Greenwald (1994) and Hanushek (1994). Other investigations of school resources, concentrating more on labor market performance, are found in Card and Krueger (1992a, 1992b), Grogger (1992), Betts (1993), and Johnson and Summers (1993). Although somewhat ambiguous, these studies suggest that specific school resources had some historical effect that can no longer be found; these suggestions are consistent with the overall reviews of resources and performance cited initially. Specific discussions of class size beyond the review materials include Glass and Smith (1979) and Word and others (1990) on the STAR program in Tennessee. The various effects of experience are discussed and analyzed in Murnane and Phillips (1981). Analyses of the use of time and its effects on school performance were developed in a background paper by Henry Levin. Specific references include Link and Mulligan (1986), Levin and Tsang (1987), Barrett (1990), and Juster and Stafford (1991). Consideration of time in school and how it is spent compared with time usage in other countries is the subject of a national report, National Education Commission on Time and Learning (1994). That report emphasizes effective use of time in school rather than simple expansion of the total time available. The overall comparisons of Japanese and American schools by Stevenson and Stigler (1992) further suggest that adding time within the existing structure would not make U.S. schools comparable to Japanese schools. Studies concentrating on differences among individual teachers include Hanushek (1971, 1992), Murnane (1975), Armor and others (1976), and Murnane and Phillips (1981); see also the policy implications of these in Pauly (1991). The individual tutoring results are analyzed in Slavin and others (1990), Madden and others (1993), and Farkas (1993a, 1993b). Discussion of union contract terms and their implications can be found in McDonnell and Pascal (1979), Eberts and Stone (1984, 1985), and Freeman (1986).

Technological innovations are analyzed in Office of Technology Assessment (1989). More extensive analyses, particularly of radio and television usage ("distance education"), are available mainly from examples in developing countries; see, for example, Jamison (1978, 1980); Friend, Searle, and Suppes (1980); Jamison and others (1981); Friend, Galda, and Searle (1986); and Lockheed and Hanushek (1988). The effects of low productivity growth on costs are analyzed in Scitovsky and Scitovsky (1959), Baumol and Bowen (1965), and Baumol (1967).

Information on spending patterns and grants to schools is provided in Garms, Guthrie, and Pierce (1978) and Monk (1990). School resources by race are described and analyzed by Boozer, Krueger, and Wolkon (1992) and Grogger (1992).

Discussions about teacher supply and teacher policies are based on the background paper by Richard Murnane. Specific analyses of supply issues are found in Weaver (1983); Goertz, Ekstrom, and Coley (1984); Murnane and others (1991); Strauss (1993, 1994); and Hanushek and Pace (forthcoming). Manski (1987) and Ballou and Podgursky (1991) discuss potential effects of overall salary increases. Various certification requirements for teachers are described in Woellner (1982) and other annual volumes. The consideration of mathematics and science teachers was originally formulated by Kershaw and McKean (1962) and has been updated in Rumberger (1987), Gilford and Tenenbaum (1990), and Boe and Gilford (1992). An example of the difficulty and costs of removing poorly performing teachers is given in Dillon (1994).

The discussions here and in the next chapter of special policies toward the disadvantaged incorporate the overall reviews and evaluations in the background paper by Henry Levin. The tutorial programs of Success for All and of Dallas are described and evaluated by Slavin and others (1990), Madden and others (1993), and Farkas (1993a, 1993b). The framework for the Accelerated Schools program is found in Hopfenberg, Levin, and associates (1993), with evaluations in McCarthy and Still (1993) and Levin (1993).

Discussion of desegregation policies is contained in the background paper by Steven Rivkin. Expenditure experiments, as implemented through court-ordered desegregation policies, are critiqued in *Economist* (1993) and Feldman and others (1994). Preschool programs and their possibilities can be found in Hill and Stafford (1974), Barnow and Cain (1977), Darlington (1980), Berrueta-Clement and others (1984), Gramlich (1986), Barnett (1992), Currie and Thomas (1993), and Schweinhart, Barnes, and Weikart (1993). Related issues on child care programs come from the background paper by Rebecca Maynard and Eileen McGinnis. These topics reappear in the next chapter.

6

Incentives:
Linking Resources,
Performance, and
Accountability

I f a single, glaring lesson is to be learned from past attempts at school reform, it is that the ability to improve
academic performance using standard, uniformly applied
policy is limited. State and federal authorities have instituted numerous regulations, spending programs, and general policy goals—all, as the previous chapter documented, to little
avail. This chapter charts an alternative course. Premised on the
evidence that no single reform is capable of solving the problems
of every school, this chapter focuses on administrative structures
designed to create incentives for each school to find and adopt
those reforms best suited to its individual situation.

If there is no single policy cure for the ills of individual
schools, then policymakers have little choice but to undertake the
daunting task of managing diversity, giving local decisionmakers
the freedom to devise educational programs appropriate to their
situation and the discipline to ensure their effectiveness. The most
appropriate, indeed the only possible place to begin promoting
diversity is at the basic unit of the school: the individual teacher
in an individual classroom.

Study after study demonstrates the importance of the classroom teacher. Estimates suggest that in a single school year an
average student with a good teacher can progress more than a full

grade level faster than an average student with a poor teacher. The same also holds for disadvantaged students. Some teachers are better at improving the achievement of children than others. Even after teachers have been through the standardization imposed by the process of state certification and school-hiring policies, large differences remain—as any parent of school-age children knows well. In truth, probably every principal and teacher in the country believes that there are important differences in the abilities of their colleagues. Yet, despite general agreement that the difference between good teachers and bad is great, few participants in the debate agree on the qualities that constitute a good teacher.

Concerted efforts notwithstanding, developing a description of "the" good teacher has defied educational researchers and educational decisionmakers alike. Several qualities, of course, seem desirable. For example, teachers should know their subject matter, be sensitive to the problems and needs of their students, and involve their students in the educational process. But this is far from a complete definition, and even these rudimentary qualities have yet to be distilled into employment criteria that ensure that teachers possessing these qualities will be hired, promoted, or kept by schools.

The simple reason for the failure to define best practice among teachers would seem to be that there is none. No single set of teacher characteristics, teacher behaviors, curricular approaches, or organizational devices guarantees a high probability of success in the classroom. Instead different teachers succeed, or fail, in very different ways. What works well for one teacher may not work at all for another, and each teacher must find the approach that best suits his or her own personality and skills and the needs of the children. One teacher may be particularly effective by employing word games with children from well-to-do backgrounds who have reading deficiencies; another may be able to motivate students by recounting personal experiences from living in Southeast Asia; yet another may be energized by close, interactive contacts with other teachers in the school. In otherwise identical situations, two teachers might apply two very different approaches and produce exactly the same level of student performance.

For that reason, detailed central regulations and directives on the nature of the instructional process and the characteristics of school personnel are bound to be wasteful and perhaps even self-defeating. So it is not too surprising that efforts by states and local school boards to improve school performance by tighter central regulation have for the most part failed.

Unfortunately, however, the overwhelming theoretical logic of the argument for more decentralized management of schools has thus far failed to work in practice. The many experiments in school decentralization have generally failed to improve student performance. The reason decentralized management has not yielded the anticipated benefits seems to be the lack of clear performance incentives, which would keep the focus on achievement even amid decentralization. Appropriately designed and consistently applied incentives appear essential to improving schools.

Performance Incentives

The strength of performance incentives is their ability to deal with complexity. By rewarding participants in the educational process when they do well and penalizing them when they do poorly, schools can harness the energy, ability, and inventiveness of individuals. The rewards to teachers may be explicit monetary rewards, or they may be a wide variety of intrinsic rewards, such as special recognition, more latitude in classroom and activity assignment, or expanded travel and training opportunities. Effective teaching is positively reinforced, and defective teaching discouraged. Performance incentives also reward effective support structures but not constraining structures.

Performance incentives are a very different approach from the current system. They do not attempt to dictate which teaching methods will work, although providing good information on what has worked in the past is an important element of any well-functioning system of incentives. Incentives encourage individuals to decide for themselves which route toward improved achievement is most appropriate in specific circumstances. Thus incentives can be viewed as a way to expand the methods for delivering a good education.

The ability to distinguish good results is crucial to any working system of incentives. Flexibility in the means of education must be balanced by crystalline clarity regarding the desired ends. This requires a highly developed ability to identify the difference between good and bad performance.

Developing and employing incentive structures is not in itself easy. As we will discuss, it requires both extensive experimentation and evaluation of the results. Failures and misstarts are inevitable, given the lack of experience with such schemes. The full advantages may come only after a substantial number of new teachers and school personnel, with skills different from those currently plentiful in the schools, have been induced to enter teaching. Nonetheless, performance incentives remain the best hope for getting on a path of long-run improvement.

Performance Measurement and Value Added

Although the details of systems that measure performance are reserved for the next chapter, one crucial point must be explained at the outset. The performance measurements used in managing incentive systems must be able to distinguish between what a given student has achieved and what a teacher has achieved with that student. Schools are but one facet of the educational process, and measurement systems must recognize—and differentiate among—the various sources contributing to student achievement.

Students come to school with differing abilities, motivations, family support, and previous achievement. A student's performance today also reflects his or her past teachers. Thus, for example, the reading performance of a student at the end of the sixth grade reflects not only the inputs of the sixth-grade teacher, but also the inputs of all previous teachers. Some families reinforce good schools. Some students are simply brighter and more able to learn and progress than others.

Any incentive system based on performance cannot ignore such differences among students. Schools and teachers should be held responsible only for factors under their control and rewarded for what they contribute to the educational process, that is, the value they add to student performance. It would be unfair, and counterproductive, to hold individual teachers responsible for the previous poor performance of their pupils.

Identifying the factors that account for differences in achievement does not and should not mean that schools either accept or condone poor performance among identifiable groups of students. Improving performance for all is the very heart and purpose of school reform. But just as accurate diagnosis is a first step toward effective cure, school officials and their management systems must be able to identify the sources of poor performance. So incentives must recognize and take into account the varying sources of differences in performance.

Alternative Systems of Performance Incentives

The current structure of schools already has many incentives built into it—as does any system of management. The problem with these school incentives, however, is that they are linked only loosely to student performance. Most teachers and school administrators are interested in the performance of their students, but, unfortunately, this performance has little to do with the rewards to the individual teacher. Instead teachers' monetary rewards and career progress are determined by other factors, such as the teachers' attendance pattern, the amount of preparation for class, and the time spent in extracurricular activities. Similar observations can be made for the incentives that apply to principals and superintendents. Intrinsic rewards are also only weakly linked to student performance in most schools.

The idea of developing stronger performance incentives directly focused on student achievement has vast appeal, and it is the subject of frequent discussion. But incentives seldom have been tried, and experiments with them have been even more limited. Recorded analyses lack many of the details crucial to judging their more general applicability. Much more experimentation will be required to find performance incentives that perform. Nonetheless, some general guidelines are obvious.

Performance incentive systems are intended to attract and retain the best teachers and administrators and to focus their energies and abilities on achieving the results that should matter most to schools: teaching students. An effective system of performance incentives will permit a variety of approaches to education. Indeed, with the same incentive system and with equal results, schools might well pursue radically different approaches, each suited to the requirements of specific students and to the talents of the school personnel. Some schools might opt for separate "academies" with integrated instruction for small groups of students; others might organize the whole school around a specific theme, such as the arts; still others might retain traditional, separate classroom instruction; some might use television to provide major parts of the instruction, combined with tutorials for individual students. A performance-oriented group of teachers and parents could choose any one of these approaches, depending on the desire and skills of the school community.

The effectiveness of an incentive system depends directly on how individuals act when faced with a given pattern of rewards. So rewards and punishments must be sufficient to get people to change their behavior, and they must be precise in their effect. Impact and effectiveness flow from the details.

Several basic frameworks, or organizing principles, can be used to design incentives. Within any of these frameworks, the precise incentive systems that are put into place may be good or bad, effective or ineffective. Although the frameworks create the outlines of improved incentive systems, the details of contracts and operations actually put into place are critical. Discovering those details should be the focus of experimentation.

The remainder of this chapter will consider two basic types of incentive frameworks. The first retains the basic administrative structure of existing school systems while altering the performance incentives for people within those systems. The second framework begins by fundamentally revising the structure of schools, to the point of virtually eliminating the current system in some cases.

Incentive Frameworks within Existing Schools

Even without changing the overall organization of the schooling system, many incentive systems can be designed to focus attention and effort on student performance. Except for merit pay for teachers, there is little experience with any of these systems, and, unfortunately, the results of past uses of merit pay for teachers have not been encouraging. The challenge, therefore, is to use today's limited experience as the basis for a program of testing and evaluating operational versions of the alternatives to determine which approaches are most useful in given circumstances.

Performance Contracting

The basic idea of performance contracting is that, instead of employing teachers and administrators directly, school systems contract with an independent firm to provide educational services to the students of a particular school. The contract might stipulate any number of things: from requiring the firm to achieve specified reading proficiencies among students to limitations on the cost of providing ancillary school services. The contractor's rewards relate directly to the satisfaction of the contractual terms, that is, the contractor is paid according to outcomes.

An early experience in Texarkana, Arkansas, in the late 1960s seemed to suggest real potential for performance contracting, but the evidence was subsequently discredited (box 6-1). More recently, Dade County, Florida; Baltimore; Hartford; and other localities have contracted with profitmaking suppliers to run some schools. A growing number of firms are advertising their desire to enter into similar arrangements. These firms are willing to compete with others and with the public schools to provide education, demonstrating their belief in the possibility of improving schools.

Box 6-1. The OEO Performance Contracting Experiment

Long-standing concerns about the education of disadvantaged students led the Office of Economic Opportunity, the operational agency for the War on Poverty, to launch an experiment in 1970 in performance contracting. Promising-looking results from schools in Texarkana, Arkansas, induced OEO to contract with private firms to provide instruction to public school students in selected sites around the country. In the end, the investigation discovered more about the difficulties of devising good experiments than the advantages or disadvantages of performance contracting.

The experiment began when OEO asked firms to bid on providing reading and mathematics instruction to a group of academically deficient students in grades one through three and seven through nine. Six firms, out of thirty-six bidders, were selected and offered very similar incentive contracts. The contract provided no payment for any student who failed to progress a full grade level during the 1970–71 academic year. Faster gains earned relatively small increases over the basic payment, and the extra payments were capped at gains of 1.9 grade levels. This incentive structure meant that both "slow" learners (likely to gain less than a full grade level) and "extra fast" learners (likely to gain near the top) yielded low returns, and might be a significant loss if they required more than average resources. Although firms could break even only when students gained 1.6 grade-level

The policy question comes down to whether or not such entrepreneurial energy can be harnessed to benefit society.

In many ways, this approach is the most straightforward example of performance-based incentives in education. The school system and the contractor define specific measurable goals, and rewards are based directly on those goals. The scope of the activity can be defined narrowly or broadly. For example, contractors can be hired to provide all educational services or a specific subset of tasks, such as remedial reading instruction. Contractors face both the incentives built directly into their contracts and the implicit threat of competition.

But in its generality, the approach begs a crucial question: what sort of contract? The success of performance contracting depends crucially on the ability to craft a good contract and to monitor its performance. As innovators in the U.S. Office of Economic Opportunity discovered, writing an effective contract is not easy (see box 6-1). And, to the extent that the contract does not fully or accurately reflect the goals of the schools, the added profit

equivalents or more, they were eager to participate because they hoped for future performance contracting business.

The very unfavorable terms of the contract led one firm to go bankrupt, two others to drop direct classroom work during the year, and all six to refuse to participate after the first year. In the end, the average performance of students was roughly equivalent to a control group that received normal school instruction.

These results demonstrate the importance of developing experience in experimentation and evaluation. Because apparently sound incentives can lead to undesirable behavior and because little is yet known about the effects of many potential policies, experimentation by state and federal governments is sensible. The fact

that many of the experiments will not improve student performance is all the more reason for systematic evaluation—so that one district can learn from another's failures instead of duplicating them.

Despite the failure of the OEO experiments, the idea of hiring private firms to manage school programs has reappeared. The Baltimore school district has contracted with an outside firm to run several of its public schools, and other districts are either experimenting with the idea or seriously contemplating it. These projects, however, are not designed as true experiments, and there is no assurance that many generalizations from these attempts will be possible.

Source: Gramlich and Koshel (1975); Schmidt (1994).

incentive of contracting firms might lead to significant distortions in the services provided. With a good contract, however, the school system can introduce competitive supply while still retaining overall authority, oversight, and fiscal control.

Charter Schools

Charter schools are a specialized version of performance contracting. School systems enter into performance contracts with outside suppliers, but in this case the suppliers are typically nonprofit institutions, at times made up entirely of existing teachers.

In 1991 Minnesota became the first state to adopt this concept when it authorized eight charter schools. In 1992 California passed an act authorizing one hundred charter schools. By early 1994 another six states (Colorado, Georgia, Massachusetts, Michigan, New Mexico, and Wisconsin) had enacted charter school legisla-

Table 6-1. State Legislation Permitting Charter Schools, as of Spring 1994

State (year)	Number permitted	Major features	Entity that must approve plan
California (1992)	100 (10 per district)	Nonsectarian; must use certified teachers; five-year contract.	Local board (with appeal to county board)
Colorado (1993)	50	Schools may not discriminate; contract for performance; various state regulations waived; five-year contract.	Local board (with appeal to state)
Georgia (1992)	No limit	Aimed at existing schools; must have approval of two-thirds of faculty; state can waive regulations with performance contract.	Local and state boards
Massachusetts (1993)	25	Business, teachers, or parents may propose; most state regulations waived.	Secretary of education (local approval not required)
Michigan (1994)	No limit	New or existing schools eligible; state board, local board, college, or university may sponsor.	Local school board or sponsor organization
Minnesota (1991)	20	State waiver of regulations; must hire certified teachers; open to all, or cross-section of population; three-year contract.	Local board (with appeal to state)
New Mexico (1992)	5	New schools not permitted; existing schools may be converted; total state funds to charter; state planning grants ($50,000) available.	Apply through local board to state
Wisconsin (1993)	20 (2 per district)	Must hire certified teachers; district can apply for waiver of state regulations.	Local and state superintendent

SOURCE: Joe Nathan, Center for School Change, University of Minnesota.

tion and several others were contemplating similar moves. (See table 6-1 for a summary of enacted charter school legislation.)

The Minnesota legislation illustrates well the basic idea. Any group of licensed teachers can propose to establish a new school; the purpose of the school can range from improving learning to using innovative teaching methods to creating new professional opportunities for teachers. A local district must agree to sponsor the proposed charter school and to be responsible for monitoring the performance of the school. The contract can last for up to three years, and the school receives state financial support. The state grants charter schools a considerable degree of regulatory relief to permit a wide variety of innovations and performance guarantees. California legislation has many similar features, and it also allows nonlicensed teachers to participate. By definition, charter schools involve decentralized school management and a greater orientation toward outcomes.

The raison d'être of charter schools is to implement teachers' innovative ideas about teaching, organizational systems for schools, reward structures, and the like. Many see these schools as a way to introduce some competition within the structure of public schools. As with performance contracting, a key element of success will be the ability to develop appropriate contracts and measures of performance. The short history of charter school experience also demonstrates some of the tensions, public fears, and potential problems with this concept. Minnesota's restriction limiting the opportunity to create charter schools to licensed teachers, for example, was a compromise balancing the risk of innovation against the interests of teachers and the desire to try something new. Other versions of charter schools also involve parents and school choice.No systematic evaluations of any forms of charter schools have yet been made.

Merit Pay for Teachers

Perhaps the most widely discussed performance incentive is merit pay, which links teachers' wages directly to their performance. Most other workers are evaluated on the basis of their performance, runs the most popular argument, so why shouldn't teachers be? Merit pay schemes strive to reward teachers who actually raise student performance. Rewards are based on results rather than behavior, and so they circumvent the difficulties in defining a priori what good teachers or good teaching might be. In practice, however, designing a workable system of merit pay has proved elusive.

Richard Murnane and David Cohen have reviewed attempts to institute merit pay, and their findings are not encouraging. Merit pay has been adopted in a wide variety of schooling circumstances, but it almost always has eventually been watered down or discarded. Subsequent analyses confirm these outcomes. School boards have generally committed little money to merit pay, leaving merit bonuses a trivial component of total teacher compensation. Indeed, merit rewards frequently have devolved into pay for extra duties instead of a bonus for quality performance in the classroom.

Teachers' unions have resisted merit pay, in part because of questions about the objectivity of methods used to measure student performance. Teachers have been particularly concerned about a school's ability to separate a specific teacher's contribution to a student's performance from the contributions made by other teachers or the student's family. A further concern about merit pay is the possibility for destructive competition between teachers. The fear is that, if teachers view themselves to be in cut-throat competition with other teachers, they might not cooperate with each other—refusing to share information about effective teaching techniques, to work together to deal with problem students, or to do public service types of activities.

These are serious issues, but they do not seem insurmountable; indeed, there are signs that union resistance is softening. After all, most other workers have some sort of merit pay scheme and do not suffer these ill effects. Their experience illustrates several factors important in avoiding pitfalls. First, shared activities should receive shared rewards. By rewarding joint achievement jointly, merit pay schemes can avoid spurring unconstructive competition. Second, the assessment and reward system should not go beyond the ability to observe and evaluate performance. Fine distinctions in performance that cannot be reliably and fairly judged should not be included in rewards. But even approximate measurement schemes still distinguish among, say, the best, the worst, and the typical performance, which enables school administrators to distinguish those who should be strongly encouraged to continue teaching from those who should be left to decide for themselves and those who should be discouraged. Third, workers must believe that the system is fair and works for them.

Many states have supported various teacher incentive plans or career ladder schemes—programs offering increased rewards to keep good teachers in the classroom. Unfortunately, the history has been one of varying state commitment, with funding being driven more by politics and budgetary pressures than by evaluations of success or failure. The general lack of systematic evaluation means that states have not been able to learn much from their attempts to develop teacher incentive plans.

There is evidence of successful use of merit pay in public employment; the Senior Executive Service of the federal government is an example. Professional teaching standards, as currently conceived, suggest an alternative in between a full merit pay system and the current use of broad certification. The teacher certification standards of the National Board for Professional Teaching Standards, when fully developed, may provide a direct and acceptable mechanism for evaluating the performance of prospective teachers. This certification, which would be voluntary, is akin to that of surgeons. Teachers would be certified on the basis of knowledge and demonstrated skills, but not on the success of their individual "operations."

The ultimate effect of any merit pay plan, if it could surmount the tremendous hurdles faced in the past, would come from two sources. Either current teachers would improve their performance in the classroom or natural selection would lead to a different and more effective group of teachers, or both. Although the evidence is not conclusive, attracting new teachers and retaining the best currently available may represent the greatest potential for improvement. Higher pay for better performance would signal teachers to move in or out of teaching, depending on their performance.

Teacher Selection and Renewal Procedures

Merit pay systems can be used to encourage the most productive teachers to stay in teaching and to discourage the least productive. These same ends can be achieved, without adopting merit pay, by changing procedures for selecting and retaining teachers. Although it is hard to generalize about the pay policies of private schools, which are unaffected by unions and most other regulatory restraints, they appear to rely not on extensive merit pay schemes for teachers, but on intensive teacher selection procedures and retention policies that link continued employment directly to classroom performance. This type of system offers a different structure for introducing performance incentives.

A key ingredient to this approach, as to merit pay plans, is the ability to assess the value added of individual teachers. Evidence suggests that principals are good judges of which teachers improve their students' performance; at least, they can identify the extremes of the distribution of teacher performance. Equally, few parents doubt that they can identify the best and the worst teachers. Current employment relations in public schools, however, limit the ability to incorporate this information about teacher performance into management decisions.

If retention policies were changed, decisions about which teachers should have their contracts renewed need not rely only on the evaluations of principals but could incorporate the input of other teachers and of parents. And, of course, any ultimate decision to fire a teacher should follow extensive efforts to improve individual teaching skills, perhaps along the lines of Japanese teacher-development efforts summarized in the comparative analysis of Asian and American schools by Harold Stevenson and James Stigler. The ultimate strength of the system would, nonetheless, rest on straightforward procedures now seldom undertaken. Active decisions would be made throughout a teacher's career about the teacher's performance. Those not performing at acceptable levels would be moved out of teaching, a fate that, today, befalls only the most grossly and demonstrably incompetent.

Any such changes, of course, alter teacher tenure rules, employment guarantees, and job expectations. Therefore, as with many other organizational changes considered here, the ultimate success of the change may depend crucially on the process of implementation. In simplest terms, any arbitrary changes in the fundamental aspects of jobs for current teachers may well lead to undesirable outcomes. These issues of implementation are discussed later.

Merit Schools

Some have proposed that, instead of rewarding individual teachers, school districts or the state reward entire schools that perform well. Such an approach would recognize the joint activities of all school personnel and avoid any possible destructive competition. Generally, these proposals envision that schools would be managed through some sort of shared decisionmaking and that schools that do particularly well would be given added resources. The underlying premise is that such a reward structure would encourage teachers and principals to set high standards for behavior, even if it did not include such powerful incentives as direct links between individual performance and pay or job security.

It is important to note that problems of measuring performance are severe, perhaps even more severe, with merit school plans than with merit pay plans geared to individual teachers. The identification of merit schools must incorporate notions of value added in the same way as the identification of merit teachers. Yet, because direct observations are more limited and comparisons less possible, merit school plans might have to rely more heavily on standardized tests and, thus, may be more prone to mismeasurement and its attendant adverse consequences. Additionally, the magnitude of incentive effects is likely to be very limited if the rewards do not include direct salary and compensation adjustments for teachers and other school personnel.

School-Based Management

An extremely popular and frequently discussed reform is "school-based management" or "site-based management." This approach transfers considerable decisionmaking from central school district

Box 6-2. Evaluations of Site-Based Management

School-based management decentralizes decisionmaking to individual schools, where teachers and students meet "to do education." Throughout the twentieth century, school districts have grown in size and become more centralized and more bureaucratic. This development has limited teachers' ability to make educational decisions, failed to capitalize on their energies, and left them unhappy with their work. With increasing frequency during the 1980s, devolution of decisionmaking to the individual school has been proposed to correct problems with centralization.

Anita Summers and Amy Johnson employed the ERIC reference system to locate evaluations of school-based management conducted from 1983 through 1993. Three results stood out. First, very little systematic evaluation has been done to ascertain any effects of school-based management on student performance. Second, and perhaps even more significant, only a few school-based management plans even listed improved student performance as a goal. Third, very few schools have any serious plan for determining whether school-based management has any discernible effects on the problems it was meant to cure.

The Summers and Johnson search uncovered more than 800 studies of site-based management (or related ideas such as participative decisionmaking or school-site management). Of these, 70 attempted to be evaluative, and only 20 used a systematic methodology. Of these 20, only 7 included any quantitative assessment of student performance, although several others included survey information, such as teacher testimonials stating that, in their judgment, "student achievement improved."

An in-depth review of the 20 most systematic studies was revealing. All of the management plans explicitly stated that greater empowerment of teachers and more

officials to principals, teachers, and, perhaps, parents. This is not an incentive framework but a decisionmaking structure, which can be operated with virtually any incentive structure. Typically, however, it has been used without any explicit incentive structure. Moreover, a review by Anita Summers and Amy Johnson argues that existing examples and proposals generally view school-based management as an end in itself, rarely linking it to student performance (box 6-2).

Not surprisingly, given the wide variety of decisionmaking procedures included under the rubric of school-based management, few consistent results about student performance emerge from existing experiments. Indeed, because altering student performance is seldom an explicit goal, performance has not been routinely evaluated.

independence for principals were primary goals. Most were explicit in wanting greater parent and community involvement. But, although improved student performance was commonly mentioned in very general terms, only 7 included specific, quantitative goals for student achievement (and of these, only 2 showed positive results). Thirteen of the 20 did not list any objective about student performance. Yet, 17 of the 20 plans involved increased resources.

This neglect of student performance is mirrored in the in-depth analysis by Paul Hill and Josephine Bonan of five major districts that employed decentralized decisionmaking in some schools during the 1989–90 and 1990–91 school years. The goals of these programs are striking in their vague focus. Columbus, Ohio, listed "school improvement" as its goal; Dade County, Florida, listed "teacher professionalization"; Prince William County, Virginia, "school improvement and public support"; Louisville, Kentucky, "school improvement"; Ed-

monton, Alberta, Canada, "budgetary and administrative decentralization." Of these systems, only Prince William County appeared to collect systematic information about student achievement (although the outside contractor evaluating the Dade County experience did include achievement scores as one element of its report).

The case study of school-based management points to significant shortcomings in setting goals and evaluating performance. Not only do the decentralizing schools not measure their own progress, but the evaluation of their experiences provides little that would help another school to decide whether to embark on similar reform. We are amazed that a policy reform that has received so much attention and support has not been accompanied by anything resembling objective evaluation.

Sources: Summers and Johnson (1994); Hill and Bonan (1991).

Economists generally favor decentralized decisionmaking in complicated organizations, such as schools, where local knowledge is important for high-quality performance. The advantages of local decisionmaking materialize, however, only when local decisionmakers have sufficient information, when the incentive structure emphasizes performance toward agreed-upon goals, when there is considerable latitude for making local decisions, and when there is a good system of accountability. Most school-based management schemes do not meet these conditions; indeed, many fail on all conditions. Some, for example, do not allow local school officials to adjust the curriculum; others bar local school officials from making decisions about hiring and firing teachers. Absent well-defined goals and performance incentives, school-based management may be worse than centralized decisionmaking.

Box 6-3. Accelerated Schools

Most attempts to deal with disadvantaged students and low achievers involve extensive remedial programs, but the results have not been very encouraging. A very different approach, developed by Henry Levin and his associates at Stanford University, starts with the premise that, instead of resorting to remedial teaching, students must be taught to do their normal lessons faster and better.

This Accelerated Schools program illustrates many of the program elements advocated in this report. The program has three key elements. First, the school must have a clear and well-articulated set of goals for student performance, agreed to by staff, parents, and students (unity of purpose). Second, decisionmaking in all key areas—including curriculum, instructional approaches, personnel, and use of school resources—is done at the school level and again involves staff, parents, and students (school empowerment). Third, the instructional approach begins with an evaluation of the strengths of students, staff, and parents, and these identified strengths in a particular school become the centerpiece of the instructional program (building on strengths). In the 1992–93 school year, the program was operating in more than three hundred schools in twenty-five states; most of the schools were at the bottom of their school district's performance distribution when they adopted the program.

Several aspects of the Accelerated Schools program stand out. At the outset the staff and parents of the school must formally accept the program, a device introduced to make sure that everybody is committed. From this starting point, however,

---

The difference between the typical school-based management approach and a system that integrates local decisionmaking within an overall economic perspective is illustrated by Henry Levin's Accelerated Schools program, which was designed to improve achievement of the lowest-performing students in a district (box 6-3). It begins with well-defined performance objectives and employs school-based decisionmaking to find approaches that meet those objectives. Regular evaluation ensures that attention stays focused on student achievement. The shared commitment to achieving student performance goals creates effective team sanctions for disinterest or nonperformance, which in turn tends to induce teachers who are not contributing to the school's efforts to seek voluntary transfers. Individual schools operating Accelerated Schools programs typically execute them in quite different ways, based on local needs and local capacity. Thus, the program embodies three of the tenets that we

individual schools can go in different directions, depending on their own views of what will and will not work. Student progress and the effectiveness of the program is measured throughout the process. Finally, the program is designed to work with very small initial additions to the school budget. Thus the program demonstrates the possibility of improving school efficiency (that is, expanding on performance for the same cost).

The expansion of the Accelerated Schools program and the local indicators of student performance suggest that it has been beneficial in a majority of the schools that have tried it. Yet very little systematic evaluation has been conducted. The national program office has put its resources into training and expansion of the program; the local schools are trying to make it work. Ideally, the federal or state governments

should organize, finance, and conduct evaluations of the programs and disseminate the results.

The few evaluations that have been conducted support the program. Studies in Houston found that students in the accelerated school improved on standardized tests in reading, language, and math, while students in the control school continued a downward slide. This and other evaluations indicate that the Accelerated Schools program is an effective model that will not suit all schools but will be effective in many circumstances. Its potential and refinement would clearly be enhanced by improved information and evaluation.

Sources: Levin (1994); McCarthy and Still (1993); and Hopfenberg, Levin, and associates (1993).

have stressed here: incentives, continual evaluation, and latitude for tailoring the program to local needs.

Altering the Basic Structure of Schools: Choice

More radical schemes of performance incentives rely on consumer choice to distinguish good schools and teachers from bad—and to reward each accordingly. Most public schools effectively have a local monopoly; parents living in a certain area have no choice over which school their children attend. Giving parents and students the ability to choose among a range of nearby schools is intended to make them more informed, involved, and influential in the education process. It would also effectively give them, rather than school administrators, the power to define a "good" education and to shape the schools accordingly.

Allowing students to choose which school to attend is meant to encourage them to attend better schools. That is a particularly valuable opportunity in inner cities, where families frequently lack the resources to move to the affluent suburbs where good schools are more prevalent. In turn, consumer choice would pressure the poorer performing (unpopular) schools to improve. Giving students and their parents a choice would thus place greater incentives on performance, because students (and presumably resources) would migrate from poor schools to good ones and force all of them to respond to the concerns of parents and to issues of quality.

Although the basic outlines are clear, choice nonetheless remains a very ill-defined term, encompassing divergent programs with very different incentives and implications. Choice provides only a general structure for schooling systems; it is the details of particular plans that influence student performance. Administrative structures falling under the general heading of choice include magnet schools, freedom of choice within a district, attendance at public schools in other districts, tuition tax credits, and vouchers good at both public and private schools. These alternatives are commonly divided into those choices that involve only public schools (magnet schools and intra- and inter-district choice) and those that include both public and private schools (tuition tax credits and vouchers). But even within these broad categories, significant variations in actual plans and their concomitant incentives already occur.

Many factors determine the effectiveness of a specific program of choice. The most important are the magnitude of resource flows, the constraints on free choice, the availability of good information on schools, the ability of parents and students to make good choices, and the scope of possible school choices. A simple example illustrates some of the issues involved. Consider a school system with two high schools. School A has excellent science teachers, while School B does not. Given a choice, students at School B who are interested in science may well try to switch to School A. One of four things might then happen. First, if School A has excess capacity, some children will transfer to it. Second, if School A is already at capacity and does not expand, no new children will be accepted, and choice will lead to no change. Third, School A could add new science teachers to accommodate the influx of students. But contract rules and district policies might enable teachers at School B, who are no longer in demand, to transfer to School A. Again, choice leads to no change. Or, fourth, School A could hire new teachers from outside. Then the movement of students could begin to have an effect, because resources would now move away from the poor school and toward the good school.

In theory, state laws that allow students to choose to attend school in another district create yet broader and more powerful incentives. In practice, much depends on the magnitude of funds that flow with students. If, for example, only state funds (and not local funds) move with students, the district losing students might have an incentive to get rid of them, but the receiving district would not have a large incentive to take in more students. The availability of money to cover the extra transportation costs of commuting beyond their local school district will affect the students' willingness to transfer. Similarly, if state law permits students to choose between public and private schools, the relative contributions to tuition made by parents, the state, and the local district have substantial implications for whether there will be any movement, whether any of the schools will see strong incentives to compete, and whether the outcomes appear justifiable.

Another fundamental question concerns the range of available choices. A basic presumption behind choice plans is that new schools—more efficient ones with better overall performance—will develop. The strength of incentives as determined by the amount of resources that accompany a student is clearly important in determining any supply response. So is the amount of regulation placed on schools. There is a real trade-off between the degree of regulation—of curriculum, practices, and standards, for example—that participating schools must face and the potential incentives these schools have to compete with each other for students. Clearly, some regulations will be needed, but regulations generally limit the range of alternatives that schools can develop. The more regulated schools are, the more any choice plan will resemble the current system.

In addition to assuming that sufficient options exist or will be developed, choice plans require that parents and students make good decisions. Although individuals are commonly presumed to be good consumers in others areas of life, such a presumption is not universally accepted in the case of schooling. Questions have been raised about whether parents will base their decisions on academic quality rather than on convenience, costs, or even the athletic programs the schools offer. The quality of the decision-making is an issue, but there is little reason to believe that parents will knowingly make bad decisions. A more important consideration is whether parents have sufficient information to make good decisions. The information routinely available about school performance is limited and distorted. Yet, in other areas consumers are presumed to make good choices only when they have sufficient information on which to base a decision. A key element of any choice plan is the provision of high-quality information about the value added of the schools, or what any school can be expected to contribute to student achievement. Not only do schools have little experience providing such information, but parents have little experience in using it to make decisions about the schools their children attend. Both must be addressed. (Moreover, while choice plans require quality information and increased decisionmaking capacity, all school reforms would clearly be enhanced by improvements in these areas.)

Deciding between public-only and public-private choice plans involves matters of trust, control, motivation, and, at times, constitutional regulation. These issues are truly important; they are also, given the lack of empirical evidence about the outcomes of choice, extremely hard to resolve by simple, conceptual arguments. On the one hand, it seems wrong to refuse to include private schools in choice programs because they, unlike public schools, are not obliged to serve all of the public. On the other hand, private schools may in fact be less responsive to the needs of disadvantaged students or may reinforce existing social structures. At a more practical level, a voucher plan could confer large windfall gains on well-off families who are currently paying to send their children to private schools.

Evidence on Choice Plans

Empirical evidence about choice plans and their effects could do a great deal to answer such concerns. Several widely publicized choice plans are in place: in Cambridge, Massachusetts; East Harlem, New York; the state of Minnesota; and Milwaukee, Wisconsin. But the evidence about the effects of these plans is sketchy and mixed, and there is even less understanding of which aspects of these plans are most important and which can be duplicated in other locations. Only the Milwaukee experiment (see below) has been subjected to ongoing, in-depth evaluation.

Because of the limited experimentation with choice, little is known about whether choice will encourage the development of new and innovative schools. For example, much of the debate about public-private choice has centered on the relative performance of Catholic schools, a discussion that assumes that, under a broad voucher system, many parents and students would choose these schools. Although Catholic schools are currently the dominant nonpublic school, they do not provide much evidence about potential supply under an expanded voucher system, or even under an open-choice charter school system. Current regulations and funding inhibit development of new alternative schools, both public and private, a situation that could be reversed if current restrictions are relaxed.

Higher education in the United States offers some lessons on this point. Unlike postsecondary institutions in most other countries in the world, U.S. colleges and universities, both public and private, compete with each other for students and resources. This competition is frequently cited as a reason why higher education in the United States is usually viewed as the best in the world. At the same time, extensive competition does not mean that all colleges and universities are of particularly high quality nor that all bad schools are driven out of business.

Choice and Disadvantaged Students

Disadvantaged students pose special problems and opportunities for the design of choice programs because, almost by definition, to be disadvantaged is to enjoy fewer choices than the rest of the population. Without special steps to enable the disadvantaged to choose as freely as their peers, choice systems may leave the disadvantaged worse off than they are now. Some fear that choice systems, particularly those that include both public and private schools, would simply turn the public schools into dumping grounds for disadvantaged and difficult-to-educate students. Some also fear that choice could increase segregation in schools. A working system of choice, however, would allow disadvantaged students to choose schools that they could not otherwise attend, either because tuition was beyond the reach of their families without the aid of vouchers or because those schools were in neighborhoods where their families could not afford to live.

Addressing these concerns and opportunities is essential in formulating choice programs. If disadvantaged students are more expensive to educate (which appears to be the case), compensatory vouchers or payments should be included in any choice plan, so that schools receive more money when they accept disadvantaged students. Regulations may also be needed to deal with possible racial or ethnic segregation. Finally, information systems are extraordinarily important in the case of disadvantaged students and their parents, who have even less experience with school choice than the rest of the population.

Choice for disadvantaged students has been the subject of an experimental policy in Milwaukee, Wisconsin (box 6-4). Milwaukee's voucher experience has not been problem free, but it demonstrates that choice can noticeably expand the opportunities for the disadvantaged. So far, evidence of higher student performance has not been found, but demand for entry into the program is growing, and parents express considerable satisfaction with the alternatives.

Indeed, a strong case can be made for wider use of vouchers specifically for disadvantaged students. Making vouchers available only for the disadvantaged alleviates the fear that the well-off will manipulate the voucher system for their own benefit. Moreover, it puts pressure on underperforming inner-city schools. Many public school districts rationalize the poor performance of their schools by blaming the requirements that they take all students, no matter how educationally disadvantaged. Providing alternative, private school opportunities for disadvantaged students—those whom public schools see as being difficult and expensive to educate— would, by their own argument, help the public schools. Vouchers for disadvantaged students would then allow the public schools to concentrate on their remaining, easier-to-educate, clientele.

Inevitably, the term "choice" has become extremely political, and support of school choice is often viewed as a litmus test for general political sentiments. Strong vested interests oppose choice systems. The most vocal opponents are school personnel, who could potentially lose job security particularly if the choice plan involves private schools. This opposition was evident in the expensive and successful campaigns to block passage of ballot initiatives that would have created choice systems in Colorado and California in 1993. The often contentious debate over choice has led both proponents and opponents to make claims that go far beyond any available evidence. As with other approaches to introducing stronger performance incentives, the idea of competition among schools creates interesting possibilities. But how effective choice can be and how to structure choice programs for maximum effectiveness cannot be known until the concept has been experimented with much more broadly than it has been yet.

Incentives for Students and Parents

Most of the performance incentives programs devised for schools have focused on teachers and school personnel. As teachers are

Box 6-4. The Milwaukee Voucher Program

In the spring of 1990, Wisconsin instituted a program to provide poor children in Milwaukee with an opportunity to attend private school. Eligible students could choose from a list of eligible private schools, and the schools would receive a payment approximately equal to the state money that would have been paid to Milwaukee public schools ($2,987 per pupil in 1993–94). This innovative plan offers unique insights into the potential for educational vouchers and for choice by disadvantaged students. The evaluation by John Witte, Andrea Bailey, and Christopher Thorn begins to describe possible outcomes of wider choice options.

Any student enrolled in the Milwaukee public schools whose family income is less than 1.75 times the national poverty line is eligible for the choice program. An eligible school has to be a private, nonsectarian school that offers no religious instruction. A participating school cannot discriminate in admission on the basis of race, gender, previous achievement, or previous behavior, and no more than half of the students in the school (65 percent in 1994–95) can be

"choice" students. If more students apply to a school than there are spaces available, students must be randomly selected. No more than 1 percent (1.5 percent in 1994–95) of Milwaukee public school students are eligible for the program. Enrollment in the choice plan expanded steadily from 341 students in the fall of 1990–91 to 742 in 1993–94. The increased enrollment appears to reflect increased participation by private schools and increasing availability of information about the program.

Evaluation of the project has included both survey work and objective comparisons between students participating in the choice program and those remaining in the public schools. These studies provide several insights. First, parents of participating students consistently cite the educational quality of the choice schools and their disciplinary environment as reasons for participating in the program. Second, choice parents start with high parental involvement in public schools and increase their involvement in private schools after joining the choice program. Third, parents in the choice program are much happier with the private school than the previous public school: 73 percent give their private school a grade of A or B, while only 48 percent

keenly aware, however, the motivation of students themselves is critical to the educational process.

Except for those aiming at the most selective colleges, most students today face only modest incentives to perform well in school. Potential employers do not have automatic access to students' grades, achievement, or even attendance records, partly because of legal restrictions. And with the expansion of college opportunities, and the dependence of colleges on tuition or state

gave their previous public school those grades. Thus, the choice program appears to be very successful in providing preferred schooling options to a significant number of poor children.

The lessons of choice, however, become more ambiguous when other performance indicators are included. First, attrition from the program is high: 40 percent, 35 percent, and 31 percent in the first three years of the program, respectively. This attrition may simply reflect the normal dropout rate for the district, but no districtwide data are available for comparison. Second, data on achievement growth (measured by standardized tests) do not show any clear gain for "choice" students in the private schools.

Whatever else the program may have done, it has strengthened Milwaukee's private school options. Even though the voucher amount is relatively low, the program has improved the financial condition of participating private schools. At the same time, the small scale of the program and the special circumstances of participating schools (notably their use of external subsidies and their ability to hire teachers at very low wages) make generalizations to larger programs or other sites uncertain. Evaluation has come at an early point in the experiment, and the experiment itself is limited to one specific version of choice. So conclusions are tentative and necessarily limited. Nothing, for example, can be said about the effects of expanded private alternatives on the public schools. Nonetheless, even at this point, it is safe to conclude that the program provides a service highly valued by some poor parents—committed parents who have a deep interest in their children's education but who lack the resources to select alternative schools. These parents are also one of the groups most hurt by the current policies of public monopoly of local schools.

An even more ambitious program of choice for low-income students was begun in Puerto Rico in 1993. This program uses vouchers that enable students to choose among public schools as well as between public and private schools, thus providing a direct incentive for public schools to compete aggressively with private schools for disadvantaged students. No performance information is currently available for the Puerto Rican experiment, and it currently faces legal challenges.

Sources: Witte, Bailey, and Thorn (1993); Bolick (1994).

subsidies, most American postsecondary institutions are not very selective in their admissions.

By contrast, many foreign countries provide strong incentives to study. In Japan, Korea, and many European countries, including France and Germany, examinations determine both the type of schooling students will receive and the careers they can expect to enter. Students in these countries work hard to prepare for examinations, and parents are heavily involved. Such examination systems are not easily transportable to the United States. In part that is because such systems limit social mobility by locking in schooling and occupational opportunities at young ages, when family influences are very important. Nevertheless, U.S. schools might learn something from studying how such systems motivate students and parents as well as school personnel.

Many foreign countries also forge direct links between schools and employers, so that a student's performance in school can have a great effect on that student's employment prospects. Such links may be particularly pertinent for schools in America's inner cities, where labor market incentives are lacking. The fact that employment prospects are little better for a student who has worked hard in school than for one who has not may well sap students' commitment to study diligently. At the same time, businesses, incongruously, frequently complain about the low achievement levels of students who seek employment with them, as if prospective employers had no effect on student performance.

Several strategies can enhance performance incentives for students. These include standardizing transcript and achievement data and making that data more available to employers, establishing better links between schools and employers, and providing better information to students about the rewards of higher academic achievement. All of these approaches make the reasonable assumption that employers could benefit from better information about scholastic performance. Only experience with closer contact and cooperation between schools and employers can show whether this assumption is generally true or could be true.

Clearly, student incentives would be even more effective if they were reinforced by better schools. Yet, stronger incentives for students can be effective within today's school system, within a school system modified to provide greater performance incentive to teachers and school personnel, and within various choice systems.

Technology and Costs

Visions of high technology schools have been painted for decades, but the reality never seems to catch the promise. The current technological vision centers on computers and flashy multimedia programs. Yet even as computers become ubiquitous, their integral position in instruction and the curriculum does not. The story behind limited introduction of technology and the remedies parallel that of school improvement in general.

With the proper incentives, technology could reduce the costs of schools in several ways. Computers can replace teachers in certain tasks, such as drill-and-practice activities. Experience with providing education through remote transmission ("distance education")—for example, the British Open University and programs in some developing countries—suggests that television and radio broadcasts, combined with correspondence materials, can provide high-quality education at relatively low cost. Broadcast education is particularly valuable in rural areas and other situations where small school populations make classroom instruction uneconomic. Broadcast education can also be used to offer advanced courses in urban and suburban areas, when existing demand cannot justify highly specialized courses. Television and other electronic educational technologies can both multiply the reach of an effective instructor and bring visually compelling programming into the classroom. Substantial relevant experience, particularly in higher education, supports the educational efficacy of these approaches.

Unfortunately, schools today have few incentives to use technology effectively. Not only are teachers not rewarded for using technology well, but using cost-cutting technology could in fact reduce the demand for teachers. Moreover, except when voters reject school budgets, school districts seldom make cost saving a high priority. The most frequent use of computers and other technological programs is to enrich the curriculum, providing presentations that are interesting and entertaining but that may not be central to the instructional program.

Incentives to conserve on costs are difficult to introduce into the current system. Expenditure control comes largely from voters and taxpayers who put pressure on the overall school budget. This pressure, unfortunately, does not readily translate into programs for introducing technological changes, particularly those that require considerable planning, training development, and capital expenditure.

One obvious way to introduce cost control pressures is through choice programs that institute competition among schools. If schools compete in part on the basis of their costs (through tuition transfers, state funding, and the like), more schools might find it in their interest to use alternative technologies to help control costs. Additionally, contracts for principals and superintendents that include incentives to cut costs could help, even within the current structure. For example, the top administrative officers of a district could receive salary bonuses for increasing student achievement at current expenditures. Such contracts are unknown in schools today.

Nurturing Experiments

Because so little is known about effective incentive systems, experimentation and evaluation of the results are imperative. The few attempts that schools and school districts have made to reform their organizations and introduce incentives have been useful and laudable, but they are insufficient in number and scope to "test" the incentive approaches outlined here. Because local circumstances are likely to influence the effectiveness of any incentive system, detailed information must be gathered about both specifics of local systems and results of the attempts. Only when the results of alternative local systems can be compared and contrasted will there be enough information to determine how implementation in different circumstances might best proceed.

Many factors, however, inhibit experimentation with educational reform. Perhaps highest on the list are the attitudes and preferences of parents. Most parents, when polled, say that, although significant problems beset American schooling, their children's schools are fundamentally sound. For them, therefore, experimenting with alternative organizations and incentives appears to be a high-risk venture without clear gains. These attitudes are reinforced, if not created, by school personnel, who find the existing system basically satisfying to their own needs. School personnel tend to tell parents that what is needed is not change, but more resources. Few school administrators or teachers wish to advertise that their school has problems other than those that can be readily solved by their newest program.

State and federal regulations and financing for schools tend also to favor the status quo. Some potentially useful innovations are flatly prohibited; others are made difficult to develop. For example, regulations on teacher certification, discussed previously, make it impossible to hire people who have not been trained in the standard manner. Requirements for dealing with handicapped children place legal restrictions on the process of education— albeit for a worthy objective, but, as mentioned, often without regard to the outcomes achieved. Special federal and state grant programs typically monitor the number of students who participate in the program but not whether the program is achieving its goals.

If experimentation is to be encouraged, state and federal governments must encourage local districts to adopt new models of incentives and organizational structures. This means eliminating regulations that prevent experimentation from taking place. But less regulation is only part of what is needed. Local districts in general do not have the expertise to design alternative approaches to schooling, and they should not be expected to do so. State and federal governments must provide better information to local districts about options and approaches. And by providing parents with information about the experiences, benefits, and risks of various experimental programs, government could help them to evaluate more realistically their own opportunities to participate in educational innovation.

To help local school districts, states might, for example, design prototypes of different incentive structures and create programs of inducements to encourage appropriate experimentation. Commitment to such an approach would be a radical departure from the current policies of most state legislatures and education departments. It would acknowledge, at least implicitly, that more of the same is not going to be effective and that, instead of controlling and mandating the details of the educational process, states would do better to improve information about alternatives and to encourage school districts to experiment their way toward their own solutions to the problems that beset them.

This approach presents political difficulties for legislators, for in pursuing it they must accept that nobody yet knows the details of programs that will improve schools. Experience shows that previous regulatory and certification approaches, which suggest knowledge of the best approach to education, have been widely ineffective. Real improvement appears instead to be promoted best by states that press for strengthened performance incentives and that support high performance goals and standards for students and schools without prejudging the method of achieving them. Doing this, however, means that instead of selling voters a solution to the problems of the schools, legislators must instead convince voters to embark on the search for a solution, a search that will require considerable effort, and some risk, on the part of voters themselves.

Still, it can be done. The remarkable history of state leadership in Minnesota provides an example of aggressive experimentation with interdistrict choice and charter schools (box 6-5). Choice programs in Minnesota now involve almost 15 percent of all students. Even in Minnesota, however, experimentation could be made more effective, and potentially more popular, if the local choice programs were clearly evaluated and the results of the evaluation widely disseminated. Today, information on educational performance is inadequate and frequently biased. Inaccurate information on performance lulls local citizens into contentment with the performance of their schools, when many should not be. Even local school personnel now find it difficult to compare their performance with that of other districts to see what they can and should be achieving.

In addition to information on the outcomes of educational experiments, local school districts will also need help in evaluating them, particularly in judging which might best apply to their local circumstances. Details are crucial: the fine print of a merit evaluation system, the rules of intradistrict choice, the appropriate range of local school decisions, and the operations of performance-based personnel systems make the critical difference in the success or failure of a particular reform.

Issues of Implementation

New systems of organization and incentives do not spring forth fully developed and fully functioning. They require long and difficult development, and these development periods are crucial for the ultimate success or failure of the experiment. If school personnel resist change or if public sentiment turns against reform, even fundamentally sound reforms can fail.

Schools often lack personnel capable of or willing to experiment with new systems of incentives. This creates a dilemma for reform-minded state governments. If they push schools into a specific "reform" or devise extensive regulations to minimize the risks of failure, they will stifle the very local decisionmaking capabilities that they are in theory striving to foster.

To encourage bureaucrats, teachers, and school personnel to devote the substantial amounts of time, energy, and resources needed to devise new programs, schools might release them from other duties, provide proper equipment and materials, and use outside consultants to foster new thinking. At the same time, states and local districts should help protect innovators from the most adverse consequences of an innovation that does not succeed. The willingness of teachers to start a charter school, for example, might relate directly to job guarantees for the teachers if the enterprise fails. If the district guarantees that teachers can rejoin the regular school system, many more teachers might be induced to develop charter schools than if they had no reemployment rights. Finding the right balance between encouraging teachers to take on entrepreneurial activity and insuring against risk is a tricky but manageable problem.

Direct performance incentives change the rewards and risks that school personnel encounter. Indeed, that is the whole point of instituting change. But those people doing well under the estab-

Box 6-5. Experimentation in Minnesota

Although Minnesota public schools had relatively high graduation rates and test scores, the state in the mid-1980s initiated reforms to improve the schools. School choice, embodied in several overlapping programs, formed the heart of the reforms. School districts were allowed to decide whether they would participate in any given program on the basis of space availability, but, once in a program, they could not select the individual students they would admit. What follows is a brief summary of major Minnesota choice programs.

—*Postsecondary Options*. In June of 1985 Minnesota's legislature enacted the Post-Secondary Options Act. This statute enabled public high school juniors and seniors to enroll in Minnesota postsecondary institutions, on either a part- or full-time basis. Tax funds followed students to pay tuition. At about the same time, the "College in Schools" program enabled high school students to earn college credit by taking special courses, offered in their high schools, that were jointly organized by high school and university teachers. By the 1991–92 school year, 7,500 students were participating.

—*High School Graduation Incentives; Open Enrollment*. In 1987 the Minnesota Legislature adopted a program to help students who had experienced educational problems to graduate from high school. Under this program such students were permitted to attend alternative programs outside their school district. More than 1,400 students were enrolled in this program at the start of its first year, the fall of 1987. Another Minnesota program allowed any student to attend school in the neighboring school district, so long as the move would have no negative effects on desegregation. Tax funds again followed students. During the 1987–88 school year, this program's first year in operation, 95 of Minnesota's 435 districts resolved to allow any student to move. These programs, plus a portfolio of other, specialized choice programs for poorly served students, enrolled 41,000 students by 1992–93. These programs

lished system are unlikely to embrace performance incentives, just as they are unlikely to embrace any change that disrupts the status quo. Teachers' expectations about career and rewards may well not be satisfied under a new system. More than that, current state laws and local regulations and contracts include explicit guarantees about wages and employment. Any new system must consider transition periods that provide safeguards to existing personnel. Although many teachers are close to retirement, teachers now in the classroom will still dominate schools for many years to come. To avoid alienating them and losing the enthusiastic participation that is crucial to success in incentive-based systems of school management, the transition rules must treat these people equitably.

appear to have induced many dropouts to return, usually to a different school, and to graduate.

—*Within-District Choice.* Several districts permit choice within-district, and Minneapolis and St. Paul even require students at certain grade levels to choose the school they will attend. A total of 67,000 participated in such intradistrict choice plans.

—*Charter Schools.* In 1991 Minnesota enacted legislation to permit up to eight charter schools in the state. Any group of licensed teachers can, with local district sponsorship, propose a school to provide innovative instruction. A three-year contract commits the charter school to meeting specified performance standards. The school must be nonsectarian, nondiscriminatory, and tuition-free (with state funding following students). The number of authorized charter schools was increased to twenty in 1993 and was scheduled to rise to thirty-five in 1994.

Minnesota's innovative programs lead the nation in establishing wider options for students (and competition among schools). By 1992–93, 14 percent of primary and secondary school pupils were actively choosing their schools (not counting those enrolled in charter schools). Other states have adopted choice programs modeled after those in Minnesota. The state's strength is its willingness to expose public school districts to more competition for students. Formal evaluation of student performance under these programs has been lacking, however. Even a half-dozen years after the programs were instituted, discussion of the pros and cons of these innovative reforms still rests on the conceptual arguments offered when they were adopted—not on evidence of whether student performance has improved.

Sources: Nathan (1989), Montano (1989), Owen (1993), Williams and Buechler (1993), Nathan and Ysseldyke (1994).

One appealing way to deal with commitments to existing teachers, while moving to radically different organizational approaches, is through two-tiered contracts. Teachers under existing contracts would continue essentially as they are now for an extended period of time, say, ten years. Basic work rules, pay structure, and the like would be maintained. At the same time, any new teachers would fall under a new contract with altered rewards, responsibilities, and risks. For example, a substantial portion of the wages of new teachers might be determined by a merit rating system, or new teachers might not have tenure rights based solely on years of experience in the local district. Existing teachers might be given the option to transfer tiers, to enter into the new contractual arrangement, perhaps with a system of bonuses for those willing to do so.

Other approaches can also be employed to recognize the implicit and explicit obligations to teachers. Direct compensation through the normal negotiation process might also be used to bring all teachers under a unified structure. Through such compromises, existing teachers can be induced to cooperate with change without restricting innovation only to those systems that existing teachers want.

Financing Improved Performance

Every state has a different approach to financial support for local schools, so the proportion of school expenditures coming from local districts and state coffers varies accordingly. Substantial variation also exists in the overall level of support for local education. Underlying each state's system is a specific notion of the public nature of education, the importance of education in determining individual opportunities, and the degree of local autonomy that should be granted.

It is a startling fact that no existing system of school finance in America explicitly rewards performance. No state gives additional funding to a district simply because student achievement has improved. Funding, in fact, may decrease, because the district may no longer be eligible for categorical grants that provide extra funds to districts with low performance. Indeed, difficulties in distinguishing between performance variations and inherent differences in the cost of education mean that some systems of finance may actually reward poor performance. Today, a low-achieving school district is invariably interpreted as a district composed of students with significant disadvantages, who require extra money for their education. A high-achieving district, by contrast, is assumed to have more educated and higher-income parents, lower costs, and less need for subsidy. Obviously, until states can and do distinguish between high-cost districts and high-performing ones, incentive systems will be crippled.

Aligning the financing system with the performance of districts would help to improve the schools. Specifically, districts that demonstrate an ability to use resources effectively should be rewarded, while those doing a poor job should not. In other words, the system of finance should be part of the incentive system that promotes improved school performance.

Improved efficiency is not the only objective of state policy, however. Equity across districts and individuals cannot be ignored. Debates over school finance, along with the related court challenges to state finance systems, have concentrated almost exclusively on equalizing the distribution of funding across districts. These discussions have generally ignored the concerns about the distribution of student achievement, the problems introduced by inefficient spending, and the true costs of providing improved education for disadvantaged students, issues that have been the subject of this work. If, however, the effectiveness of district spending were improved through, say, some combination of the outcome incentives described here, the questions of equitable distribution of funding would take on new importance. Simply put, when money can be counted on to be spent effectively, the distribution of spending will be directly related to the distribution of student achievement—and society will have to deal directly with the implications of any funding disparities.

Increasing equity and instituting performance incentives at the same time may introduce additional complexity into reform efforts. Certainly, it would be undesirable, and perhaps unconstitutional, if districts with the wealthiest families were to receive the largest subsidies because their performance improved the most. Rewarding performance need not mean abandoning equity, however, and systems can be created that achieve both objectives.

The Essentials of Performance Incentives

No matter what their field of endeavor, people respond to incentives. Because the incentives in schools bear little relationship to student performance, it is not surprising that schools have not yet improved student performance, despite constant reform pressures. Several programs are available that would connect incentives to performance—either by linking teachers' and administrators' pay directly to some objective measure of the results they achieve with their students or by letting parents and students themselves decide which schools best meet their needs and therefore most deserve their support.

Establishing programs that embody such incentives presents many challenges. Much more experience is needed to determine which incentives will work in which circumstances. The transition from today's system of school management to a more incentive-based system presents potential difficulties in maintaining the cooperation and involvement of existing school personnel, who may feel threatened by change. Ways must be found to reconcile the common need to promote change from the top with the local, decentralized decisionmaking that makes incentive-based systems most effective.

All of this calls for dramatically different roles for everyone now involved in education. Of prime importance is a redefined role for state and federal officials. These levels of government will have a diminished voice in specifying how education is to be delivered. But they will play a much greater role in promoting and inspiring the changes to be undertaken by local districts, in setting objectives and goals, in evaluating performance, in encouraging the adoption of new technologies, and in providing information to local districts. In short, their role changes from manager to coach. At the same time, local school officials and teachers will have to take a more active role in decisions about costs, structure, and curriculum. Instead of simply following instructions from above, personnel in each school will effectively have to create their own educational system. Many incentive systems also call for greater parental involvement in the educational process. Incentive-based systems can promote diversity where it is needed. And, should a single panacea for schools prove possible after all, incentive-based systems provide the strongest possible motivation for its quick, universal endorsement.

Bibliographic Notes

Evaluation of differences among teachers comes from Hanushek (1971, 1992); Murnane (1975); Armor and others (1976); and Murnane and Phillips (1981). Pauly (1991) emphasizes the importance of variations within schools because of differences in individual approaches and teacher performance. Committee for Economic Development (1994) integrates ideas of performance incentives with the governance of schools and the decisionmaking capacity of states and local systems. The quantitative magnitude of differences across teachers comes from Hanushek (1992). The description and evaluation of early performance contracting efforts and experiments is found in Gramlich and Koshel (1975). The most recent introductions of contracting by for-profit firms are analyzed in Schmidt (1994). Current thinking on charter schools can be found in Randall (1992), Amsler (1992), Williams and Buechler (1993), Diegmueller (1993a), and Nathan and Ysseldyke (1994). An extensive evaluation of merit pay systems is found in Cohen and Murnane (1985, 1986), is reinforced in Hatry, Greiner, and Ashford (1994), and is also discussed in the background paper on teacher supply by Richard Murnane. An annotated bibliography of work on merit pay can be found in Karnes and Black (1986). American Federation of Teachers (n.d.) and Shanker (1993) put forth the views of one teachers' union on evaluations, merit pay, and the like. See also National Board for Professional Teaching Standards (1991). Cornett and Gaines (1994) provide a useful summary of state incentive systems and career ladder plans as they have evolved during the 1980s and into the 1990s. Inferences about supply effects on the quality of people who enter teaching come from Manski (1987); Ferguson (1991); Murnane and others (1991); and Hanushek and Pace (forthcoming). Direct evidence on the ability of principals to evaluate the value added of teachers comes from Murnane (1975) and Armor and others (1976). Site-based management is reviewed in the PEER background paper by Summers and Johnson. See also Hill and Bonan (1991). Accelerated Schools are described in Hopfenberg, Levin, and associates (1993), with evaluations in McCarthy and Still (1993), Levin (1993), and Henry Levin's PEER background paper.

Choice is the subject of a wide range of publications and journal articles, including a special issue of the *Economics of Education Review* 11 (December 1992). Vouchers were proposed in early writing by Friedman (1962). See also Coons and Sugarman (1978) and Lieberman (1989). Nathan (1989a, 1989b) and Nathan and Ysseldyke (1994) discuss many of the attempts to institute school choice. Clune and Witte (1990) provide a series of articles on the theory of choice (vol. 1) and discussions of experiences with choice (vol. 2). Chubb and Moe (1990) present the case for vouchers for low-income students, along with empirical analyses related to school bureaucracies. Carnegie Foundation for the Advancement of Education (1992) provides a critique of choice, and, in turn, is critiqued in MacGuire (n.d.). Witte,

Bailey, and Thorn (1993) evaluate the Milwaukee plan. The Puerto Rico choice program is outlined in Bolick (1994). Lieberman (1994) provides an interpretation of recent voting on choice initiatives. The history of Minnesota's experience with public school choice is found in Montano (1989), Nathan (1989a), Nathan and Ysseldyke (1994), and Owen (1993). International experience is reviewed in Glenn (1989).

7

Turning Schools Themselves into Learning Institutions

That school administrators should regularly evaluate the achievements of school programs seems obvious. Yet schools have seldom made any serious effort to assess the performance of either existing programs or major innovations. This failure poses fundamental problems for performance improvement in general. How can schools hope to improve systematically without ascertaining what is and is not currently working?

Innovative programs for schools come from a variety of sources: education schools, policy institutes, textbook publishers, teachers' unions, individual district program offices, and teachers and principals themselves. Individual schools and school districts may adopt these programs for many reasons, from resolving a crisis to improving an already successful organizational structure, and they may adapt the program to fit the particular local circumstances. Once they have put programs in place, few schools make any serious effort to gather information about how well they are working—unless they are obviously broken.

Two reasons underlie this reluctance to judge. The first is that defining success in schooling is hard. Intuitively, school personnel have long resisted standardized testing and assessment. Instead of using a fixed set of criteria to evaluate students, educators have preferred more flexible systems that allow each student to emphasize his or her own achievements. Yet flexible measurement quickly degenerates into a collection of semi-independent observations and impressions that cannot be compared. The second difficulty in assessing schools is establishing responsibility and developing appropriate accountability. Even if some measurement of performance is accepted, using it to assign praise or blame is difficult because so little is understood of the inner workings of the education process. Schools, as we have repeatedly stressed, are just one part of education, and schools themselves are complicated institutions involving many components.

Evaluating the past effectiveness of school programs is difficult enough, but the reforms we propose add new challenges for evaluation. The performance incentives proposed in the last chapter would move schools into uncharted waters. Instituting such reforms would demand a commitment to evaluation unlike any that has ever before existed in education. Moreover, if progress is to occur at an acceptable pace and with an acceptable amount of uncertainty, new approaches to developing information will be necessary.

At a minimum, successful evaluation will require new leadership from state and federal government to help create measurement techniques, to develop ongoing evaluations, and to disseminate accurate information. In describing the new roles of governments in the last chapter, we underscored the need for experimentation with alternative incentive schemes. A well-designed program of experimentation and systematic evaluation of the components of incentive schemes will lead to more rapid accumulation of knowledge. But, beyond that, explicit attention to random assignment experimentation, described below, offers even greater possibilities for learning. These evaluation approaches nonetheless require significant changes in the way the business of education is conducted.

Some argue that improved student testing and assessment can lead reform by itself. With accurate assessments of student performance from tests, runs the argument, schools will automatically focus on improving test scores: teachers will adjust to improve student achievement, management decisions will become obvious, and reform will occur almost spontaneously. We know of no evidence to suggest this is a realistic expectation. We wholeheartedly support the development of higher standards and improved measures of performance. But we doubt that they will be good enough in a variety of relevant dimensions to carry reform.

Two parallel developments are necessary to improve the ability of educators to evaluate the school system. A systematic approach to experimentation and evaluation of school programs must be developed and instituted, and the assessment of student achievement must be refined and improved. These two facets of improving the knowledge base are obviously interrelated, but they can be most clearly understood if discussed separately.

Finally, it must be underscored that virtually no progress will occur without regular measurement of success and failure. Indeed, a primary reason for believing that school reform is necessary is that available measures of student performance trace the problems. Although some would minimize or discard evidence from existing standardized tests, perhaps arguing that conceptually superior measures should be used, it would be a mistake to do so without an operationally useful alternative. Existing measures of performance, although flawed in some ways, still can provide useful information about the success of schools, programs, and approaches. The suggestions that follow below about various improvements, particularly for direct use in incentive plans, should not be interpreted as a wholesale condemnation of existing tests for evaluative purposes. Instead these proposals outline a plan of development and improvement.

The Varied Uses of Performance Assessments

Historically, schools have concentrated their assessment efforts on the progress and performance of individual students. Course grades, written comments on student development, and, more recently, performance on standardized tests all provide information on how well each student is doing. These assessments are based both on absolute standards, such as whether the student meets certain specified learning goals, and on relative standards, such as how the student compares with peers in the classroom and across the country. These assessments give teachers information they can use to develop educational strategies for both groups and individuals.

Individual assessments also create incentives that motivate students to study. A key factor in the strength of those incentives, however, is the degree to which assessment information is made public and used to judge the student. Promotion through the grades, graduation, and the like constitute an important part of the public's general knowledge about individual students, providing strong incentives for them to perform well in those terms. Scores on standardized tests and course grades are sometimes used to make judgments about students, for example in the college application process, but frequently they are not made generally public, thus lessening the incentives for students to perform well. Employers virtually never review student transcripts, so course grades consequently hold less importance for many students.

Assessments of student performance have uses in addition to shaping students' careers. Most obviously, they can and should be a part of both new and existing efforts to evaluate the programs teaching those students. Reforms designed to introduce performance incentives heighten the importance of program evaluation and student assessment. If rewards are linked to student performance, teachers, principals, and other school personnel can more clearly focus their efforts on the prime task of education. But such linkage requires accurate and consistent evaluation of performance, which is relatively uncomplicated and inexpensive to provide. It also requires assessment techniques that are subtly, but importantly, different from those used to measure students. Comparing the performance of a student to the other members of the same class is one thing. Comparing the performance of that class, as a group, to peers across the nation is harder. And assessing the contribution made by individual teachers and administrators to that performance is harder still. Yet all three types of assessments must be done if reform is to drive forward.

Key Ingredients of Performance Measurement
for Management

The ultimate point of evaluating education is to improve the management and operations of schools by providing both a grounding for policy decisions and incentives for teachers, students, and other school personnel to perform well. As such, assessments will inevitably be controversial, for they not only affect the careers of those in the schools, but they also implicitly define the objectives of the school system.

A good assessment must be linked to the objectives of the educational system. As with many aspects of education, though, this apparently simple requirement is much easier to state than to implement. Many school goals are imprecisely defined, and, therefore, are not very helpful in designing measurement systems. Many educators who try to make the goals more specific tend to be overly inclusive; school objectives come to touch upon every conceivable aspect of life and learning and are thus cumbersome to use in the day-to-day management of schools. Pennsylvania's attempt to adopt an outcome-based education system, for example, illustrates many of the problems of achieving consensus on manageable goals for schools (box 7-1).

There are two natural starting points for creating educational goals and developing techniques to measure progress toward them. One, now most commonly used, is to build upon the objectives of the school curriculum. When states define school programs, most stipulate the courses the students must complete and the material those courses must cover. Implicitly, these objectives define what a student must achieve to move on to the next grade. These goals form an obvious starting place for assessment.

A second, often neglected, starting point for setting educational goals is career skills. For most students and their parents the raison d'être of schools is preparation for useful and rewarding careers. So the acquisition of job skills is an obvious candidate to be represented in performance assessment. Job skills, however, should not be viewed simply as those taught in the traditional vocational education courses. Indeed, the evidence suggests that

Box 7-1. Outcome-Based Education in Pennsylvania

In 1990 Pennsylvania's state board of education began a review of its regulations on curricula, instruction, and assessment. Frustrated with the results of earlier attempts at school reform, the board proposed the idea of outcome-based education, following an emerging national trend favoring the evaluation of schools based on the performance of students, as opposed to school inputs (such as course work).

After countless hearings and meetings, the state board of education in March 1992 voted to make Pennsylvania the first state in the nation to adopt a statewide policy of outcome-based education. Months of protests and delays ensued. The board eventually approved a list of fifty-five educational outcomes in January 1993. Instead of following a fixed curriculum, students would be required to meet each of these outcomes to graduate from high school. Only one

month after the agenda was approved, however, Pennsylvania's House of Representatives voted overwhelmingly to nullify the outcome-based regulations. Finally, in summer 1993 a new, reduced set of objectives became the governing objective for Pennsylvania schools.

Proponents of Pennsylvania's outcome-based education believe that eliminating input regulations will improve schools by allowing them to focus on student achievement. By giving teachers and administrators flexibility in devising curricula and instruction, reformers hope to encourage the creation of innovative strategies to meet the high standards set for students and to use resources more efficiently. Finally, they argue that focusing on outcomes provides greater accountability.

Conversely, opponents of outcome-based education believe that the reform is too drastic a change to be undertaken without any valid research to support it. They believe that some of the board's outcomes fo-

the career skills most highly demanded in the labor market are general communication and analytical skills, logical reasoning ability, and the like. These are general skills that all students should be taught and that should also represent the core of assessment systems. In addition, schools can and do improve parenting skills, make citizens more informed voters, discourage crime, and the like. Such external goals may also play a part in assessment and evaluation, although care need be taken when extending goals beyond academic and career skills to avoid creating measurement systems that are unworkably diffuse.

In addition to focusing on the objectives of schooling, a good assessment plan must be consistent and precise. To be useful in managing schools and providing incentives for school personnel, assessment schemes must separate the effects of schools from other

cus on student attitudes and values rather than on cognitive ability and that it is not the state's business to meddle in those areas. Moreover, even the academic outcomes are defined very vaguely, giving teachers, textbook writers, and test developers little guidance. Opponents further argue that assessment systems, newly developed to measure student performance, are too subjective and expensive and that provisions for remedial education are insufficient. Because outcome-based education eliminates course work requirements that ensure that schools offer certain subjects, opponents fear that some schools will reduce their curricula. Moreover, outcome-based education could require less effort of top students. The net effect, say the opponents, will be to lower educational performance rather than to raise it.

Pennsylvania's experience amply demonstrates the potential problems that arise when schools shift to outcome standards. To begin with, the program has not been completely developed and has not been demonstrated to be reliable enough to drive the entire system. The incentives for good performance and the sanctions for bad performance are largely undefined, making the efficacy of the system uncertain. Finally, the system is based heavily on the development of strategic plans by districts and on the certification of these plans by the state board of education, but there is no evidence that either group has sufficient capacity to do these well. Thus, although the sentiment behind the state's outcome-based education policy is consistent with the recommendations of this report, the state may have created insurmountable problems by introducing the system without first having done some experimentation and evaluation.

Sources: Rothman (1993); Harp (1993); Diegmueller (1993b); Pennsylvania State Board of Education (1993); Ravitch (1994).

factors that also influence student performance. Teachers can be confronted with students who are unprepared for any number of reasons: inadequate previous schooling, lack of motivation, little help from parents, or physical or mental limitations. Teachers may perform their own jobs better if they are aware of these other factors, but teachers should not be evaluated on factors over which they have no control. Similarly, allowance should be made for schools that receive ill-prepared students. In other words, the evaluation must allow assessment of value added by the school and teacher, that is, assessment of precisely what the schools contribute to the student's learning. Too often evaluators look only at absolute performance levels, instead of the value added.

Central-city schools, for example, are frequently condemned as failures without considering the overwhelming problems they face. Even the best teacher may not be able to transform an inner-city seventh grader reading at the fourth-grade level into an eighth grader reading at the eighth-grade level. Nonetheless, a teacher who could bring that student up to the sixth-grade level by the end of the year would be doing a spectacular job, even though the improvement would not be sufficient to overcome the initial deficit. Just the opposite occurs in many affluent suburban districts, where the high level of achievement the student initially brings to class may mask poor teacher performance. The schools in these areas willingly take credit for the high absolute level of their students, even though their value added might be low.

High overall performance must be the final goal, but the best way to achieve that goal is to evaluate and reward programs, teachers, and schools according to what they contribute to individual student performance. Measures of total levels of performance will inevitably include influences outside of the school's control.

Forms of Testing and Measurement

Much of the current controversy about performance measurement in the schools revolves around student testing. Tests are alternately seen as a useless administrative burden, as a comprehensive force for low standards and mediocrity of schooling, or as America's best hope for driving performance improvements through reluctant school administrations. All of these views have some validity. Done well, however, testing has a crucial role to play in the process of learning about education that is the heart of school reform. The challenge is to ensure that testing is done well.

Standardized Testing

In recent years standardized tests have assumed an ever larger role in evaluating student performance. Many states now require periodic examinations using standardized tests. Data on average performance on those tests, broken down by district and often by individual schools, are frequently made available to the public. The availability of such information and the attention paid to it in the media and elsewhere has led to intense debate about the usefulness and appropriateness of standardized tests as a measure of school performance.

Properly done, standardized testing offers a level of objectivity and comparability that is unavailable from other sources. By applying a universal yardstick of student achievement, such tests have obvious advantages over other, subjective evaluations of performance. Tests can be used to evaluate differences in achievement among groups of students, say, in several schools with different programs. They can also indicate patterns of change in achievement levels.

The use of standardized tests, however, can also lead to unreliable conclusions about student performance. Many different tests are available, and the question "what to measure?" is one of the most contentious issues in standardized testing. To know what skills to measure, schools must first decide what skills they are seeking to produce. For example, a well-constructed test of Urdu might indicate which students knew that language, but, without a consensus that all students should learn Urdu, the test provides neither an overall assessment of educational achievement nor the basis for a comparison of achievement among schools. Consensus on the overall goals of American education has, at least in the past, been elusive. The future may be better, however, as efforts to develop national goals and standards begin to pay off.

Widespread testing entails hazards as well as difficulties. High-stakes testing, such as that required for high school graduation, where the results are perceived to have strong effects on students or school personnel, can lead to several unproductive outcomes. Teachers may emphasize material expected to be on the tests to the exclusion of all other material. Schools may overtly distort the results by selecting only certain students to take the tests. Some schools are even rumored to have misreported results of student examinations.

The final, and most common, complaint about standardized testing is that many available testing systems do not accurately measure the range of material and skills that should be taught in schools. By overemphasizing testing, teachers and administrators neglect more complicated or creative tasks, which are not easy to test but which are still important to their students' education. Research on the accuracy of standardized tests is ambiguous, but addressing concerns of inaccuracy should form a key part of a program designed to use standardized tests more effectively. Such a program should consist of four parts.

First, research should be devoted to defining more clearly just what skills and achievements standardized tests should attempt to measure. This effort should be broadly based and solicit advice of people outside the standard schooling and testing groups, such as businesses. Second, because the range of items that can be tested effectively is limited, standardized tests cannot be the sole measure of performance. Other measures need be designed to complement standardized tests, particularly when the tests are components of a reward system. Third, because existing tests are subject to misuse and can bias instruction in undesirable ways, extreme caution must be exercised in rewarding teachers and school personnel for high test scores. Although results of standardized tests might form part of the evaluation of teachers, exclusive reliance on test results is likely to damage the quality of teaching. Downplaying the importance of scores is not particularly limiting to teacher evaluations, however, because principals are able to identify good performance without relying on test results. Fourth, test performance for individual students must be traced over time so that growth in achievement, instead of the absolute level of achievement, becomes the object of attention.

Although many have looked to testing to play a crucial role in driving reform, today's standardized tests cannot fulfill the reformers' high expectations. Current testing is not sufficiently accurate to pinpoint differences in the achievement of individual schools. More important, differences in school curricula make standardized measures hard to devise. Broad tests, of the kind that can encompass the inevitable differences in goals and emphasis from school to school, do not provide accurate and detailed data about differences among teachers and their classroom performance. Particularly in the near term, at the level of the school and classroom, more direct evaluation by the principal (and perhaps teachers and other personnel) is likely to provide more accurate information.

At the same time, standardized tests remain one of the best instruments for programmatic evaluation available today. Standardized tests can provide objective comparisons of basic skill development that facilitate hard decisionmaking about what is and is not working. These tests can be improved, but their usefulness for evaluative purposes is undeniable.

Authentic Tests

To overcome the difficulties of standardized tests, several educators have recently embarked on new and diverse approaches that promise richer views of student performance. Whether it is called "authentic testing," "genuine testing," or "performance-based testing," this approach is based on the notion that open-ended responses to standardized tasks and questions will allow better assessment of a student's true performance levels. Short answers, essays, math problems without multiple-choice answers, and more creative activities, such as writing poetry or personal narratives, form the basis for such assessments.

In addition to painting a better picture of an individual student's abilities and skills, authentic testing can also more effectively measure the broad range of analytical tasks that schools should be developing. Indeed, the time-honored tradition of individual evaluation within the classroom uses a similar approach. Such testing permits the teacher to make more precise assessments of the strengths and weaknesses of individual students.

Experience with authentic tests is limited, and work on many facets of such tests is in its infancy. Therefore, much of the current discussion is based on speculation and extrapolation of what might be developed. Clearly, authentic testing will always be more expensive and time-consuming to administer and evaluate than standardized tests based on multiple-choice responses. Thus, any

---

Box 7-2. Vermont Portfolio Scores

Vermont introduced an innovative assessment system in 1988, when it began exploring the use of portfolios of a student's best work in mathematics and writing. That system is now employed statewide in grades four and eight. Although the program has been in effect for a limited period, early evaluations of its successes and failures provide useful insights into the use of portfolios and other types of authentic tests.

Because it previously had no statewide assessment system, Vermont wanted to use its new program both to provide information on student performance and to encourage improved teaching. In mathematics teachers construct portfolios of five to seven pieces of the student's best work covering puzzle solving, applications, and investigations. In writing teachers choose six to eight different pieces, such as poems, short stories, and personal narrations. Each portfolio is submitted for scoring by other teachers. There are also objective examinations of certain content areas, although these are not necessarily multiple-choice examinations.

The Rand Corporation evaluated Vermont's portfolio assessments in 1991–92 and 1992–93. These evaluations concentrated on the reliability of the ratings of the portfolios. In simplest terms, did different evaluators rate the same pupil in the same way? And did evaluators consistently rank different aspects of each pupil's work? In the first year of evaluation, which corresponded to the first year of statewide implementation, reliability was very low on both mathematics and writing. As shown in the table, the correlation of writing scores between different portfolio raters was only 0.6, although that for mathematics reached a more acceptable 0.8.

---

potential gains will have to be compared with the added costs. The General Accounting Office has estimated that authentic tests might typically cost about twice as much as multiple-choice tests. The higher cost can be easily justified, however, if it results in more accurate measurements of student performance and in improved school efficiency.

Larger concerns about authentic testing center on the comparability of scores, both among groups of students and over time. Because the scoring of most authentic tests is subjective, many question the reliability of any resulting quantitative summary. Some uses of testing do not require explicit quantitative scores, however. For example, individual teachers do not necessarily require such information. Reliability is an important issue when performance measures are used to compare students in different schooling situations as part of an assessment of the effectiveness

	Writing		Mathematics	
Grade	1991–92	1992–93	1991–92	1992–93
Fourth	0.49	0.56	0.60	0.72
Eighth	0.60	0.63	0.53	0.79

High rater reliability is, however, a minimal requirement for good assessments. The right things must be measured. The overall congruence of portfolio scores with the desired outcomes for mathematics and writing is unknown. This issue, validity of the assessments, was not fully evaluated because of the low reliability of the scores.

The Vermont experience shows that widespread use of portfolios appears administratively feasible. It does come at a cost: ten to fifteen hours of classroom time a month go into developing portfolios, significant teacher preparation also occurs, and other direct resource expenditures for training and evaluation are required. Part of this time is clearly spent on legitimate student learning activities, but part represents a true additional burden on the teachers and on the class time of the students.

The Vermont experience also demonstrates that classroom instruction can be integrated with the assessment system. The amount of time required to train teachers to use the system is likely to be sizable, however. Further, explicit definition of what is desired is a necessary precursor to obtaining changes.

The assessment experiment has yet to demonstrate whether it is cost-effective. Furthermore, the program was not designed to assess individual student performance, and whether it can do this is unknown. As the program is currently structured, unraveling information about the value added of schools or programs appears impossible.

Sources: Koretz and others (1993a, 1993b, and 1993c).

of schools, for example. Vermont's full-scale use of portfolio testing, a specialized form of authentic testing, provides mixed evidence about the reliability of such devices, although an entire testing project has not yet been completely developed (box 7-2). The same issues and questions arise over using authentic tests to measure the value added of teachers and schools to the progress of individual students.

The (often offsetting) advantages and disadvantages of standardized and authentic testing suggest that schools should consider using a combination of both. The choice of which to use in any specific situation depends on the kind of information needed. For detailed assessment of student performance, authentic testing offers clear advantages in the depth and richness of data. For overall assessments of the educational system involving direct comparisons of performance, standardized, multiple-choice tests may offer equally clear advantages, particularly when measuring basic skills and analytical ability that have been shown to fit into standardized testing approaches.

Other Performance Measures

Although measures of cognitive skills are a central element in assessing the performance of schools, other important measures include a school's graduation rate, the percentage of graduates that attend postsecondary schooling, and the job prospects of graduates. Schools are also expected to develop important social values.

Although they should not be ignored, schools' contributions to progress toward these other objectives is profoundly hard to measure. Specifically, it is very difficult to separate the effects of the school and its teachers from other factors. For example, family income strongly influences college attendance. Changing admission and financial aid policies of colleges and of governments lead to changes in college attendance over time, even when schools provide the same training. Similarly, the strength of local economies influences whether students continue in school or seek employment. Separating the influence of schools from factors outside the control of schools is more difficult in these areas than it is for tests.

Similarly difficult is identifying which specific programs and teachers were instrumental in developing particular skills that are observed only after the student has left school. Because supplying labor markets with better-skilled workers is a primary reason for improving skills, identifying the educational programs that best prepared students for the world of work would be useful—but it is seldom possible. The inability to link programs to actual outcomes prevents long-term measurements of the effect of schooling from being used to evaluate specific educational policies. Although useful in setting goals for preparing students for subsequent careers, alternative measures are not now capable of assessing the performance of the school system.

National Standards and Testing

During the past decade, increased emphasis has been put on developing national goals for student performance and on ways to test whether these goals are being met. Together these efforts define minimum, but high performance objectives for graduating students—a national consensus of expectations for the achievements of students and schools. And by creating such a consensus, the promoters of national standards hope to remedy one of the identified shortcomings of educational policy: that schools and teachers do not know exactly what is expected of students and, thus, of them.

The best example of the development of national standards is found in mathematics, where mathematics educators have developed specific goals for student achievement (box 7-3). What they have not yet produced, however, is a technique for measuring progress toward those goals. Nor does anyone yet know how instruction might ultimately change as teachers and schools attempt to meet these goals.

Not surprisingly, efforts to create national standards for schools have proved controversial. Apart from concerns about the validity of testing associated with national standards, one of the primary arguments against national testing is that it will reduce local control of schools. If national standards are imposed and if testing relates to these national goals, so the argument goes, local districts will have no choice but to follow the national notions of what schools should be doing, instead of meeting standards laid down by local school boards and parents. Such concerns seem overstated. Although local control is portrayed as the historical norm, in fact local control of schools has been steadily eroding for some time. State governments in particular, but also the federal government, already impose goals, curricula, and even details of instructional programs on local districts. The National Assessment of Educational Progress, a continuing effort to measure performance at different ages for a representative group of U.S. students, is in essence a form of national testing that has existed for two decades, and the SAT and Advanced Placement tests can

Box 7-3. Standards and Testing—The Math Experience

Along with demand for improvement in overall learning has come a call for new, challenging standards of performance. So far the most developed—and most acclaimed—effort to develop specific standards for education has been in mathematics. The Mathematical Sciences Education Board of the National Research Council (MSEB) and the National Council of Teachers of Mathematics (NCTM) have collaborated since the mid-1980s to produce several, increasingly detailed reports on specific content standards for mathematics at different levels.

Experience with mathematics standards illustrates several important issues. The MSEB has developed three general principles for linking assessment to effective education: the content principle (assessment should reflect the mathematics that is most important to learn); the learning principle (assessment should enhance mathematics learning and support good instructional practice); and the equity principle (assessment should support every student's opportunity to learn important mathematics). Throughout, the development of standards has been linked to the development of measurements.

But there is a snag. Beyond general principles, linking content standards to measurement is very difficult. Papers commissioned by the MSEB suggest that no one has yet developed accurate methods for assessing whether students are meeting the package of mathematics standards. Furthermore, there is no assurance that instruction

be considered de facto national examinations for college-bound students.

A great deal of local control of education is clearly essential, particularly if performance incentives are to be emphasized. But local control need not, and should not, extend to modifying or overriding minimal goals for student performance set nationally. Students must compete in a national, if not international, market for jobs. In promoting economic development and social mobility, the nation has a legitimate claim to set minimal goals for all students to compete in this national job market.

Less conflict occurs in fact between national goals and local control than would seem the case at first glance. Under most reform plans local districts would be responsible for developing specific educational approaches, designing incentive systems, and meeting the special needs of local populations. But the idea that each locality should follow its own approach to education does not conflict with the idea that the students attending these schools

will change so that students can be expected to learn what they need to know to
meet the standards. Lynn Hancock and Jeremy Kilpatrick review analyses of how testing affects instruction. Although many suggest that "what you test is what you get"—
that is to say, teachers will spend a large
part of class time simply preparing students
for the test—the evidence is less clear. Students always learn more than is tested and
do not learn everything that is tested. Stephen Dunbar and Elizabeth Witt offer a
further caution about testing and assessment linked to new standards. Expanded
standards for mathematics, they argue,
raise new questions about the reliability
and validity of existing methods of measurement.

The experiences of those developing
mathematics standards and assessments
lead to two conclusions. First, it is possible
to develop much more specific and appealing definitions of desired learning outcomes
than currently exist. Second, the hope of
assessment-driven reform of schools is
overly optimistic, because existing methods
of assessment are not advanced enough for
the task and because new methods take
considerable time to develop. Improved assessments will continue to be an important
element of program evaluations, but they
are unlikely by themselves to lead to sufficient changes in teacher incentives and behavior.

Sources: National Research Council (1993);
Hancock and Kilpatrick (1993); Dunbar and Witt
(1993).

should all reach a standard, minimum level of achievement, nor
do national minimum standards prevent localities from developing
their own, more stringent standards.

A less high-minded reason for opposing calls for national
testing is the reluctance of some school officials to have comparisons made among schools. This concern is justified to the extent
that schools are unfairly held responsible for things outside their
control. But if national examinations were designed to permit the
unraveling of the value added by schools, comparisons would be
reasonable and beneficial. Only if school performance in areas
agreed to be important is accurately measured can education make
progress.

National measurement of achievement is threatened not only
by outright opposition, but by indifference and by attempts to
divert the energies now focused on measuring performance into
national programs to increase educational resources and inputs.
Many school officials do not see much use in national standards

and testing, because individual districts are more concerned about their own specific programs and student performance than about comparisons with other districts and students. They are thus prone to argue that money spent on national tests would better be spent on actual delivery of educational services.

To complement national performance standards, some propose "opportunity to learn" standards, which would establish national minimum levels for the resources used in teaching students. Such standards would be not only unhelpful, but also potentially damaging. Today's tenuous understanding of the links between school resources and performance make it impossible to define precisely what resources would be needed in a given situation to achieve the national educational goals. So resource standards are likely to promote further inefficiency through mandating inappropriate resources. More insidious, some see this movement as delaying the development of good measures of actual school performance.

Evaluation Approaches and Randomized Assignment Experimentation

In theory, the quality of schooling can be assessed simply by comparing the performance of students in one program with otherwise identical students in different programs. The problem, of course, is that there are no "otherwise identical" students; students and circumstances vary across programs in complicated ways. Nonetheless, programs can be evaluated by using statistical methods that combine a wide range of information on students and their schools to isolate the key differences in programs through detailed description of all the separate factors. Applying these statistical approaches correctly is the trick.

The bulk of information about programs, incentive structures, and the like necessarily comes from direct analyses of the programs as they are operated by individual schools. Variations in school districts provide a rich array of experiences. States can work with several school districts, or even schools within a single district, to try deliberately to test all interesting variations of the details of programs and incentive mechanisms. This approach can deepen the schools' understanding of the factors affecting school performance by showing how changes in program details affect overall results.

Schools should also make greater use of an alternative approach, randomized assignment experimentation, which is a method for separating the effect of a specific aspect of treatment from other factors. Medical researchers have made great advances through such experimentation, even when they do not completely understand the underlying physiology of given treatments. The idea is simple in concept but frequently difficult to carry out reliably. The key element is selecting students for specific programs entirely by chance. If done properly, the only systematic influence on performance between those in one program and those in another will be the program itself.

Suppose, for example, that one wants to study the effect of smaller classes on student achievement. If researchers simply look at performance in the large and small classes found in a typical district, they cannot be sure whether any observed differences in student performance come from the effects of class size or from the specific students and teachers in the different classrooms. For example, if the school principal attempted systematically to provide small classes for the students performing at the lowest level, performance might appear to be lower in the smaller classes, even though that is actually not an effect of the smaller classes per se. To overcome such problems, students (and teachers) could be randomly assigned to classrooms with varying numbers of students, which would reduce the chance that preexisting performance differences would bias measurements of performance by class size. The STAR program in Tennessee used this approach and found further evidence of the general ineffectiveness of smaller classes (box 7-4).

The STAR example also highlights some of the potential difficulties with randomized experimentation. To be appropriate for random assignment experimentation, the program or educational intervention must be well defined and capable of being replicated

Box 7-4. Project STAR

The Tennessee state legislature funded an unprecedented school experiment in 1985 relating to class size. Early reviews by Gene Glass and Mary Lee Smith of the effects of class size on student performance suggested that reducing class size produces only minimal benefits until classes shrink to fifteen students or fewer a teacher. Before investing in a costly policy of reducing class sizes, Tennessee decided to commission its own study of the effectiveness of smaller classes.

The program, named STAR for "Student/Teacher Achievement Ratio," was a four-year randomized experiment. Students in seventy-nine schools across the state were randomly assigned to a small class (13–17 students), a regular class (22–25 students), or a regular class with a full-time aide. The experiment included students in kindergarten and grades one through three, and participating schools had to have enough students to have each type of classroom. At the end of each grade, students were given Stanford Achievement Tests in reading, math, listening, and word study skills; at the end of grades one through three, they also took the state's Basic Skills First (BSF) test of reading and math.

The results indicate that students in small classes perform better than those in large classes for kindergarten and perhaps for the first grade. In the second and third grades, small classes made no difference in achievement, after allowing for the initial achievement differences at the end of kindergarten. Students in regular-size classes with aides did not perform significantly better than classes without aides.

The STAR program illustrates the type of experiment that can uncover information about basic organizational issues. The ran-

in many different settings. Class size is appropriate for such experimentation, because variations in size are easy to define and because even fairly small districts have sufficient numbers of classes so that variations in size can be introduced. Conversely, the effect of state teacher certification requirements, say, in the number of courses in pedagogy that are required of prospective teachers, is difficult to evaluate using randomized assignment because the certification requirements apply across an entire state; changing requirements for individual districts would interact with the hiring practices of those districts, making any observed effects difficult to interpret. Additionally, educational experiments are bedeviled by student mobility. The full effects of educational programs generally take some time to evolve, but maintaining randomly assigned programs for students who have moved to a new district or observing their achievement as they progress through school is difficult. Thus, randomized experiments are an appro-

domized experiments, which involved selecting a random set of students and assigning a random teacher to each type of classroom, attempts to overcome any unmeasured differences among students and teachers that might distort achievement gains.

The experiment also illustrates the difficulties of such experimentation. The initial differences in kindergarten achievement could reflect important gains from the use of small classes in the earliest grades, but, because students were not tested at the time of their initial assignment, the differences could also reflect problems with the random assignment of students. The results were probably also limited because achievement differences among students in classes of fifteen would still be fairly small (according to Glass and Smith), compared with those in larger classes. Finally, experimental difficulties associated with student mobility

and with the participants' knowledge of the experiment have unknown effects on the results.

The experiment cost about $3 million a year. This amount, while large in terms of evaluation projects, is small compared with the costs of reducing class size in the state. For example, in 1987, Tennessee had 42,000 teachers. If reducing class sizes from twenty-two to fifteen required hiring 30 percent more teachers, the additional one-year salary costs would be $300 million (not counting any fringe benefits). If just elementary school class sizes were reduced, the added annual cost would still be close to $200 million. The results of the STAR experiment suggest that most of these additional expenditures would be wasted.

Sources: Glass and Smith (1979); Word and others (1990).

priate and valuable tool that should be used more extensively, but they cannot be the only method of evaluation.

Because of the technical, theoretical, and political difficulties of more comprehensive evaluations of school performance, undertaking testing programs is a task that only the largest and most sophisticated school districts may be able to do on their own. So the higher levels of government have a clear role to play.

Governmental Responsibilities

State and federal governments, like local school districts, exhibit a distinct lack of enthusiasm for evaluating schools—even though from their broader perspective they would seem to have much more incentive to do so than districts, which have always focused on educating students. These governments have done only limited amounts of systematic analysis and evaluation. Traditionally the federal government has undertaken sufficient evaluation only to justify reauthorization of its primary programs, such as compensatory education funding or Head Start. It has done little in areas outside of the programs it funds. States themselves have not taken on a very broad role in evaluation.

The task of developing and providing information about alternative educational approaches should be part of the primary mission of federal and state education departments. Knowledge about the performance of specific programs or incentive plans can help to guide the decisions of all districts in the country. Many approaches that involve substantially different operating procedures cannot be fully evaluated by looking at only a single district. And the complexity of the educational process itself makes evaluation of even simple programs difficult. Highly skilled and specialized personnel are often required if an evaluation is to be done properly, and most local districts will not, and generally should not, attempt to develop complete evaluation offices. Each of these factors bolsters the case for state and federal provision of evaluation services. State and federal education agencies should also disseminate the results of the evaluations. These agencies are in a position to see a broad range of options. They also can produce the relevant information for broad groups of consumers.

Nonetheless, two obstacles stand in the way of a more productive government role in the evaluation of education. First, local districts are not always eager to have state and federal officials involved in local activities. Second, as described previously, the most useful long-run information will come from observing the outcomes of a variety of organizational structures and incentive programs. Although some variation in incentive structures might happen naturally across districts, it most likely would not be varied sufficiently to provide precise information about effectiveness. Each of these difficulties will call for a new compact between state and local districts, which will need to cooperate more fully in designing and evaluating innovative incentive programs. Inducements to persuade local districts to cooperate may be necessary. The districts may find participation in experimental programs too difficult or time-consuming, and they may be unwilling to risk having ineffective programs exposed. Reversing those traditional attitudes on the part of local districts is one of the challenges and necessities of reform.

The Burden of Testing and Evaluation

Although the potential benefits of more comprehensive testing generate considerable enthusiasm, the burden of testing and evaluating creates considerable concern. Testing students takes time, and schools frequently express doubts about whether additional testing would be worth the time and money. Current testing programs do not appear to be excessive; an average of fewer than four hours a year is spent in testing for all students, although testing for some students in some years can get noticeably larger. As with all other forms of educational expenditure, testing is justified only when the benefits exceed the costs.

Today, school districts can and should use tests directly to help with the selection, design, and reform of educational programs. Testing could also provide more and better information about the results of programs from other districts. Future testing should be done with a specific purpose, and testing programs should themselves be evaluated by state and federal governments. Used more diligently and intelligently, testing could become not a burden, but the foundation of a program of experimentation and learning to educate educators about education: what works, what does not, and what could work better. Such a program offers the United States its best hope of comprehensive education reform.

Information for Parents

It is common to lament the fact that parents are not more actively involved in the schools and that some do not show much interest in their children's education. One reason for this parental neglect is the minimal amount of information parents ever receive about schools. Parents have little hope of making informed judgments about the quality of alternative schools or programs. Without more and better information, parents cannot participate effectively in school decisions, even at the level of voting for school budgets.

Improved school evaluation could provide parents with the information they need. Indeed, some reforms would require parents to have better information and to participate more actively in schooling. For example, school choice programs would not work if parents had to make choices based only on currently available information. Without better information about performance and achievement across schools, choices would likely revolve around issues of race and social status—pushing the results of choice programs in very undesirable directions.

Institutional Learning

Schools invest remarkably little in information about their own operations. Compared with that on private industry, the amount of research and development on schools is minute. So also is the amount of resources and energy devoted to quality assurance in schools. More than that, school personnel are accustomed to think that evaluation of programs and activities is unimportant, more a nuisance than a necessity.

In contrast to teachers' own behavior, this attitude is even more remarkable. Teachers continually evaluate their students, knowing that such information is invaluable in determining whether a student is meeting objectives, having difficulties with material, working sufficiently hard, and being properly prepared for the future. Teachers have few qualms about evaluating students in areas where objective measurement is exceedingly difficult, from social skills to attitudes.

Schools themselves must actively learn; continuing the unchecked drift of the past quarter century is simply untenable. Schools, like their students, must be subjected to systematic measurement and evaluation. The information generated by this process must in turn be employed to direct the course of development of the schools.

Bibliographic Notes

A general discussion of conceptual issues related to testing in schools is found in Office of Technology Assessment (1992) and American Educational Research Association (1985). The importance of measuring value added and the distortions from not doing so are described in Hanushek and Taylor (1990); Steuerle, Meyer, and Hanushek (1991); and Meyer (1993). The importance of improved basic skills was outlined in chapter 2 and is reinforced in recent policy statements such as Marshall and Tucker (1992) and Committee for Economic Development (1994). Interpretations of standards, assessments, and test results are also given in Wirtz and others (1977), Breland (1979), Congressional Budget Office (1986, 1987), Hartigan and Wigdor (1989), Koretz and others (1991), Bishop (1991, 1992), National Council on Education Standards and Testing (1992), Medrich and Griffith (1992), Shanker (1993), American Federation of Teachers (n.d.), Commission on the Skills of the American Workforce (1990), and Ravitch (1994). The importance of linking high standards to needed workplace skills is vividly described in Commission on the Skills of the American Workforce (1990) and Marshall and Tucker (1992), along with many of the preceding sources. Standards-driven systematic reform is discussed in Smith and O'Day (1990), and its potential effect on the disadvantaged is addressed in O'Day and Smith (1993). Congress in April 1994 passed HR 1804—Goals 2000: Educate America Act—establishing formal national goals that build on previous work done by the governors. Pressures to modify standards because of failure are identified by Shanker (1994) and Harp (1994). Mathematics standards and testing is discussed in National Research Council (1993). New designs for tests and information on their time and cost is discussed in Dunbar and Witt (1993), Koretz and others (1993a, 1993b, and 1993c), and General Accounting Office (1993). Effects of teaching and school practices are reviewed by Hancock and Kilpatrick (1993), Koretz and others (1991) and Koretz and others (1993c). A simple discussion of the use of random assignment experiments in related areas can be found in Ashenfelter (1987). Results of the Vermont portfolio assessment are found in Koretz and others (1993a, 1993b, and 1993c). Evidence about class size from the Tennessee STAR program is developed in Word and others (1990).

8

Improvement: Necessary and Possible

We believe, together with many others, that improvements in U.S. schools are necessary, if Americans are to reach their highest potential as individuals and as a society. When it comes to specifics of methods and approaches to improvement, however, we advocate an approach quite different from that found in most of today's school reform discussion. Instead of pushing a single program of reform, we urge experimentation focused on explicit incentives for improvement and systematic evaluation. And we do not believe money is the answer. Reform will come more assuredly from an improved decision process that focuses attention on student performance than from further attempts to overwhelm the problems of schools with resources.

The High Priority of Improvement

The United States devotes substantial resources to schooling, and it should reap maximum benefits from that expenditure. Annual public spending for elementary and secondary education now amounts to about 3.5 percent of gross domestic product, a figure that, for a variety of reasons, may well grow during the next decade. Another 1 percent of GDP is devoted to public spending on higher education, and the productivity of those expenditures is directly affected by the quality of the students entering the nation's colleges.

During this century improvements in the education of the population have made important contributions to the overall performance of the economy. The U.S. economy has been the envy of the world, as productivity advances have pushed the nation's income and wealth to unexcelled heights. But, more recently, slowdowns in the expansion of the amount of education received and stagnation in student achievement have contributed to a slowing of economic growth.

Halted progress in the educational system has come just as business and industry are demanding an ever more skilled group of workers. Intensified worldwide competition in goods and services forces businesses both to improve upon their procedures and to cut costs if they are to survive. Productivity gains have historically been largest when new equipment and highly skilled workers combine to create more efficient production techniques. Without a labor force capable of adjusting to new demands, businesses in the United States will lose markets to foreign competitors.

To be sure, the U.S. economy will continue to be strong far into the future, even if no improvements are made in the educational system. The nation begins with a strong economic base, and its flexible economy can work around some of the effects of a less qualified work force. But the result of current trends is likely to be an economy different from one created with the help of a strong educational system. An inefficient educational system produces less-skilled workers, less-sophisticated products, and eventually slower economic growth and a lower standard of living for the American population. And the educational system itself will absorb more resources than need be, distorting the investment and consumption decisions of society.

As important as education is for the nation as a whole, the effects of education on individual opportunities are even clearer and more compelling. Education translates directly into improved earning opportunities for individuals. The past two decades have seen a veritable explosion in the relative wages and salaries of the highly educated, while the least educated are left farther and farther behind. The education-related earnings gap is largest for the newest entrants to the labor force, apparently reflecting an intensified competition for the most-skilled new workers. This demand also bodes ill for today's least-educated youth; they are likely to earn low wages throughout their lives.

Opportunities for income mobility, a hallmark of American society, are closely tied to the leveling effects of quality schools. The powerful influence of family background on student achievement, coupled with the close link between educational achievement and economic success, suggests that society will become more class-ridden and stratified with a mediocre education system than with a good one. If inadequate education confines poor and minority children to inferior labor market opportunities, the United States will find itself with a rigid social structure, unlike any of the past.

What Is Missing, What Is Needed

Efforts to reform U.S. education have continued unabated for a decade. The outpouring of concern, strategies, and objectives is truly impressive. Yet, virtually all of this work has either neglected or downplayed two factors that we believe are absolutely critical: efficiency and incentives.

—*Costs and Efficiency.* People interested in school reform seldom explicitly address the costs of new programs or calculate whether benefits will be sufficient to outweigh the costs. This neglect causes important problems. Schools and decisionmakers should always remember that there are other uses for any funds. Public and governmental support of schools depends crucially on a sense that money spent on schools is well used. Benefit-cost analysis is the best way to provide such assurances. This is not an abstract, conceptual idea. Instead, it is a commitment to ensuring that clear and identifiable returns result from added resources.

The logic of comparing costs to benefits applies not only to new programs but also to existing ones. Schools historically have been averse to evaluating programs and to analyzing the cost-effectiveness of different policies. Not coincidentally, there is ample evidence that inefficiency reigns in today's schools. If they could reduce or eliminate that inefficiency, most schools would immediately discover extra funds that could be channeled into new programs and ideas.

—*Performance Incentives*. By attempting to change schools through one-size-fixes-all programs, through new certification requirements and regulations, and through nondirected instruments, such as overall salary increases, reformers frequently fail to mobilize individuals in the schools to perform well. Indeed, many traditional models for schools create conflicting pressures that might even undermine performance. Although school reform efforts are increasingly focusing on performance, the current organization of schools pays little attention to the incentives that teachers, administrators, and students face. The reality is that these incentives are only weakly linked to student performance. Teachers receive about the same rewards whether their students do well or poorly. Moreover, most reform proposals pay little attention to the structure of incentives.

In our view, the only real hope for improvement comes from strong and clear performance incentives. By rewarding individual people and schools for outstanding achievement, administrators can encourage the school system as a whole to match that achievement.

No Magic

Basing their theories on speculation and extrapolation rather than on what is known from reliable, documented experience, reformers have too frequently suggested simple answers and promised quick and decisive improvements in schooling. But the problems that face America's schools are not simple, and it would be foolish to believe in easy victories.

At the heart of many discussions of school reform is an unshaken belief that providing more resources will allow schools to improve performance. If only the nation could extend the school year, reduce class sizes to permit more individualized instruction, or pay teachers more, this line of thinking goes, then it would see quick and decisive signs of heightened student performance. But these approaches have been tried, and they have not worked.

Nor has taking a specific educational approach or program that appears to work in one place and transporting it with equal success to another. Tellingly, few successful curricula or teaching approaches remain successful from one era to another. This lack of staying power reflects the difficulty in moving programs from one context to another and is instructive for the approaches suggested here. Incentive plans such as performance contracting or school choice, for example, come in many different designs, and they face a varied landscape of schools with different kinds of students, teachers, and parents. Mandating choice or insisting on a magnet school in every moderately sized district may work in some places but not in all, perhaps not even in most. Why? Largely because there is insufficient understanding of the details of the interactions between such incentive programs and their environment. Critical details are lost in the transition, resulting in failure. More important, there is no reason to suspect that the details necessary to direct a radically improved system through centralized regulation will be uncovered anytime soon.

A bias against evaluating the success or failure of a program perpetuates today's limited understanding of what exactly determines success in different times and places. With new programs being instituted year after year throughout the country, educators could potentially learn a great deal, and they might use experiences from past attempts to improve future ones. Over the long run, the quality of information about schools will dictate the possibilities for the system as a whole.

Setting Realistic Expectations

Adjustments and changes to school programs short of outright reform will occur continually, as they have occurred throughout the twentieth century. But these naturally occurring changes are unlikely to produce lasting and important changes in the educational system as a whole. Under the current systems of incentives and evaluation, schools do not seem much more likely to adopt approaches that work than those that do not work. Not to introduce performance incentives and evaluations is tantamount to endorsing the current system of marginal change, a continuation of the process that has led nowhere in the past. Moreover, it is important to design approaches that encourage risk-taking behavior, to try out a wide variety of new schemes.

At the same time, expectations of what reform can accomplish need to be managed to be more realistic. In the past, programs frequently have been oversold, apparently reflecting a perceived marketing requirement that only the loftiest goals will gain sufficient attention to be introduced into schools. For example, in mathematics the average nine-year old in the United States is performing two or three years behind the average student in several other countries. It is inconceivable that the United States could climb to scoring highest in the world on mathematics tests by the year 2000. Yet that was one of six goals for American education that the nation's governors developed in 1989 and that Congress adopted in 1994. Surely, emphasizing the importance of mathematics skills is valuable, as is observing that U.S. students are not keeping up with students from other countries. But an expectation that any policy put in place in 1994, or even in 1989, could lead to such an enormous change by the year 2000 is unrealistic and almost certainly will result in dashed expectations.

Fundamental improvements are possible, but they will come slowly, and they will be accompanied by various local failures along the way. To have unreasonable expectations about both the pace of change and the setbacks is to constrain the possible changes and, perhaps, undermine the entire enterprise.

Experimentation and Evaluation

History clearly suggests the possibility that current incentives, coupled with the cost structure of schools, will doom education to steady deterioration. Regulatory approaches, such as those designed around certification requirements or state mandates, offer little hope because their success depends on finding simple uniform solutions to the problems of schools—a task that requires more information than any educator now has and that may be downright impossible. Moreover, expanding current programs implies spending ever increasing amounts on highly skilled personnel just to stay at the same point, because other sectors of the economy can afford to offer increasingly higher salaries to the skilled people whom the nation needs as administrators and teachers in its schools.

Although private industry has experimented with many systems for evaluating and rewarding personnel, the public sector has little similar experience to draw upon in developing its systems. Competitive companies in the private economy are constantly being pushed to do better. Those firms that do not develop systems of incentives and rewards and that do not adjust to new demands ultimately cannot compete with other firms; eventually they are swallowed up by better-managed firms or go out of business altogether. Firms thus continually monitor their own operations to judge which approaches are most productive. Schools have been nurtured in the public sector, which has been insulated from, if not immune to, outside pressures. Experimentation and entrepreneurship, the keys to economic success, have played virtually no role in schools.

Public provision of schooling is not incompatible with proper incentive structures, even though public schools have not done much yet with performance incentives. Schools are generally reluctant to try new approaches for several reasons: public decision-makers do not like to take risks; teachers and other school personnel resist changes that might change the way they do their job or threaten the job altogether; parents are reluctant to put their children in experimental educational programs. But, as documented, the public school system is not functioning well now. It is not keeping pace with the demands of society for increasingly well-trained citizens and workers. And it is not providing good return on additional public money invested in schooling. Therefore, the possibility that some experiments with incentive structures do not ultimately succeed should not stop all efforts to try new things. On the contrary, failure is, in a sense, already the status quo in education.

One additional reason for reluctance in trying new incentive structures deserves special attention. Past efforts at revising the structure and activities of schools have seldom been subjected to serious and thorough evaluations. Indeed, learning about what does and does not work is not a central issue in most school systems. But when programs are not evaluated, it is clear that experimentation is much less likely to lead to any long-term improvements, making experimentation itself less likely. The value of encouraging experimentation with different approaches is diminished dramatically if schools do not follow a consistent and coherent method for evaluating the results of that experimentation.

Evaluating different programs, modes of operation, and incentive structures is not a simple task. At a minimum, improved measurement techniques are required. Without a system capable of measuring improvement, there is little chance of making decisions that improve the overall system. But measuring only performance is insufficient. Evaluation requires that new systems be compared with the existing system, and such comparisons are often difficult to make in actual operational situations. The chief difficulty is disentangling the new program from all the other factors that simultaneously affect student performance.

Two aspects of evaluation have received insufficient attention. First, the primary responsibility for developing the knowledge base about the effectiveness of programs should fall on federal and state governments, not local school districts. An important aspect of learning about schools is developing a database on successful and unsuccessful approaches that can be disseminated around the country. A local district will not have the proper incentives to do a thorough evaluation, because it is less concerned with how students in a distant district perform than with how its own students perform. Therefore, once a local district has decided to adopt a plan, it has limited interest in thoroughly documenting its implementation for the use of other districts. Moreover, few local districts are likely to invest any of their limited resources in employing and developing sophisticated evaluation units, again because their primary business is educating students, not providing information about which programs are most effective and why. The local district has a mandate to ascertain whether its resources are being well spent, but this mandate stops short of extracting larger lessons about overall reform of the system.

Second, more attention should be given to truly randomized experiments. The medical profession, faced with incomplete knowledge about how the body functions, has made tremendous progress in the treatment of diseases by testing proposed treatments on one group of randomly chosen people while withholding such treatment from another, allowing a simple comparison of results to indicate efficacy of the treatment. Even if the biochemistry of a treatment is not understood, doctors can begin fighting a disease once they have obtained information about how it reacts to a given treatment. That such an approach is seldom attempted in education perhaps helps to explain why educational science has lagged far behind the extraordinary progress of medical science.

Random assignment experimentation is not without risks. The treatment might be ineffective, preventing the experimental subjects from receiving a more efficacious treatment. The treatment might have side effects or might actually be harmful. The researchers might be misled about what specific aspects of the treatment are working. Because of these dangers, many potential subjects are reluctant to enter into an experiment. And, indeed, it is common for parents to say, "You cannot experiment with my children. We are not going to have you risking their future with an experiment that may or may not work."

These concerns are justified, and they demand attention in the design of any experiment, in education as well as in medicine. Strong ethical guidelines are necessary, as is a coherent strategy for designing particularly effective experiments. Nonetheless, random assignment experimentation is a valuable tool, particularly given the limited understanding of the educational process. Trying new structures may solve the serious problems in the existing system of education. Parents may cling to the status quo, not realizing how ineffective it is and how much can be accomplished with innovation.

Public Schooling and Incentives

The historic conflict between ensuring the availability of public schooling and preventing the distortions of monopoly was long ago resolved in favor of insulating schools from outside pressures. Free access to schools is a long and important national tradition in the United States, and the nation's achievements have been admired worldwide. Yet, ensuring access to schooling does not imply that incentive structures should not be altered.

Incentives internal to the public school system can be altered without threatening the existence of public schools. There is no necessary link between the current organization and structure of public schools and the existence of a strong public school system. To be sure, some schools and some school personnel would find that they were in less demand if the focus was turned to performance. Yet, even if private schooling were expanded, which is an optional, not a required, element in changed incentives systems, a strong public school system is still possible. And change can no longer be avoided without serious damage to our schools.

Students and Parents

Education is not solely the responsibility of schools. The effort individual students devote to their schooling is obviously an important ingredient. Parental attitudes about the value of education and the direct educational inputs of parents and siblings also influence individual students' academic performance.

Incentives should be developed to encourage students and parents to participate more actively in education. Many students do not see directly the value of higher achievement, particularly if it takes additional effort. Employers evaluating students for new jobs seldom consider the academic achievement of the student.

They virtually never request or receive a student's transcript or the more detailed recommendations of teachers. The incentives are also reduced for those students who want to go on to highly competitive colleges but who are satisfied to attend one of the many noncompetitive postsecondary schools that admit students regardless of their academic performance in high school.

Most parents have an interest in the success of their children. But, once their children are performing within a broadly acceptable range, too many parents see muted incentives for improved academic achievement. Pressed by other demands on their time and energies, parents are frequently willing to let schools assume primary responsibility for their children's learning. Indeed, with more single-parent families and working mothers, schools are increasingly pushed into acting as parent substitutes.

Strengthening the incentives for students and parents to participate more fully in the educational process is important and worthwhile. Much more could be accomplished with more active studying at home. Sometimes parents are unsure about how they can help. If parents do not know what they can do to support the schools, to motivate students, or just to help with homework, it may be possible to provide them with useful information. Still, mixed past experiences in helping parents to help students reemphasizes the need for experimentation in education. Nobody has yet developed broadly useful "information packets," or parental education programs, for widespread distribution. On a smaller scale, however, specialized programs for disadvantaged students, such as Accelerated Schools or Success for All, do appear to be effective in improving parental interactions with students. More needs to be known about how to encourage strong student and parental involvement in the schooling process.

Developing specific mechanisms and incentives to promote greater parental involvement in schools is difficult. If the prospects of better jobs and higher educations do not motivate parents to help students to succeed in school, other incentives may not be very effective either. The nation cannot merely mandate more parental involvement. Some approaches to educational reform will compel parents to improve their effort, but any such mechanism is likely to produce mixed results: parents who already have a strong interest in schooling are likely to increase their efforts if encouraged to do so, but those who are less interested at the outset react little. Unfortunately, this differential effect frequently reinforces existing rigidities and problems. Children already getting little support and encouragement generally remain unaffected by new outreach efforts.

Altered incentive structures for schools should lead schools to be more interested in the various factors that influence student performance. Today, schools look at family backgrounds and outside influences on students more for their use in rationalizing disappointing performance than for their potential to guide the design of new approaches. This situation could well change with emphasis on student performance.

Nonetheless, the lack of viable policies to improve education in the home requires reformers to concentrate on schools, which can be directly changed by public policy. Even though schools are not solely responsible for student performance, they are inevitably the appropriate focus of policy attention. We can implore parents to be more involved, but we cannot rely upon it.

Attracting, Selecting, and Retaining Quality Teachers

The single most important input to schools is dedicated and able teachers, and efforts should be directed at ensuring that such people enter and stay in teaching. Attracting and retaining the best is, however, exceedingly expensive, and perhaps impossible, if, in setting salaries or renewing contracts, schools are unwilling to make judgments about who is performing well and who is not.

Schools are not now very good either at encouraging the best potential teachers to enter teaching or at retaining the best performing teachers in the system. They are quite effective in spending more money on teachers, however. For example, when schools now grant tenure and increase the pay of all teachers (regardless of their performance), they accomplish nothing in terms of improving student performance, even though they increase expenditure substantially. Although general wage increases expand the pool of potential teachers, there is little evidence that simply expanding the pool leads to significant improvements in student achievement. To do that, schools will have to institute new procedures to identify, evaluate, and reward teachers according to teaching ability.

Almost all school systems already have some sort of evaluation system for teachers in place, although the weight given to actual performance in the classroom varies. But even systems that emphasize classroom performance make minimal managerial use of this evaluation information. It might form the basis for some recognition of achievement by the principal, for teacher counseling, or even for in-service training of teachers. Very seldom does it determine anything about pay, retention, tenure, or other similar incentives.

Moving to a system where performance directly affects a teacher's compensation and retention is extraordinarily difficult. Besides questioning the fairness of any evaluation system, teachers are quite legitimately concerned about any new system that radically alters what they have come to expect from their job. Because they accepted their current jobs with clear expectations about work conditions, compensation, and rewards, contractual obligations, both explicit and implicit, are present.

Two-tier arrangements represent one means of dealing fairly with existing teachers while developing improved incentive structures for new ones. Current employees might be "grandfathered" under existing employment arrangements, while new teachers are hired with very different contracts. Current teachers (and principals) might also be given options to join the new system, perhaps even encouraged to do so by the promise of a bonus on joining. Still other approaches are also possible.

Any educational reform must take great care to retain the goodwill and willing involvement of teachers. Education depends critically on teachers and their interactions with students. Teachers are not another input into the education process that can be easily replaced. Individual classroom teachers make many of the most important decisions in education, and their involvement in the process is indispensable. Many "top down" reforms, where teachers are simply told what to do, start from a position of disadvantage and deteriorate quickly as teachers become increasingly alienated.

Teachers who are unwilling or unable to participate in reform should not be ignored, but neither should they be allowed to hold up progress. The politics of recruiting and motivating teachers to participate in reform proposals is one of the trickiest, and most crucial, elements of reform.

Collecting and Assessing Performance Information

Evaluation of educational performance is the subject of intense debate, or, to be more precise, intense debates, for there are many issues in the discussion. First, few school systems conduct systematic evaluation of performance; many continue to do only sporadic testing. Policymakers, parents, and educators are increasingly demanding more and better information on the performance of schools. At the same time, psychometricians and others who develop and analyze measurement instruments debate the validity and usefulness of many common tests. According to some, many of the most frequently used standardized tests of cognitive achievement are overly simplistic and, if given too much importance as a measuring tool, prone to distorting the activities of schools. This perspective has fostered a deeper discussion of goals and standards for schools and the subsequent measurement of progress toward them.

Part of the problem with testing clearly results from a lack of specific goals for schools and students. If the objectives of schools are not clearly specified, measuring their performance is obviously extraordinarily difficult. Yet setting goals and standards for schools is the subject of its own debate. Some argue that national goals in education would impinge on local and state prerogatives. Others argue that goals might be unfair to school systems that, because of a variety of disadvantages, could not realistically be expected to meet them.

Although some states and localities might wish to take goals and performance standards farther than the rest of country does, specifying high minimum national performance goals for schools and subsequently measuring how well schools are meeting the goals are imperative. The United States cannot hope to develop its national potential and to have a truly world-class work force without a clearly defined—and heavily promoted—set of objectives for education.

Perhaps the most lasting effect of the past decade's reform discussion will be the recognition that education is a national problem that requires a national solution. This recognition is contained in federal legislation on educational goals passed in 1994. The development of national goals began with the nation's governors, was carried forward by a Republican president, and was written into law by a Democratic-controlled Congress and a Democratic president. The importance of this bipartisan effort should not be underestimated.

The next challenge is to translate the goals into clear, strong, and reliable performance measures. The second challenge is to link these measures to an organizational structure to achieve the goals—or at least to ensure consistent movement in the direction of the goals.

The skills that should become the centerpiece of the national goals are fundamental cognitive skills: high levels of literacy, analytical ability, and scientific knowledge combined with the ability to reason abstractly. Too much past debate about national goals has fallen prey to disagreements about moral standards, individual attitudes and perceptions, and specific behaviors of students. These are important matters, which schools have an active part in developing, but measuring and improving school performance cannot be deferred until Americans reach agreement on morality and other issues outside the realm of general cognitive skills.

The movement toward high standards for student performance has been propelled in part by a notion that these standards could be the centerpiece of reform, that schools and teachers would naturally and more or less automatically adjust their behavior to meet the goals. The reality of the process by which standards are developed, by which assessment instruments are developed to match these standards, and by which teachers modify their approach to accomplish the goals suggests that fulfilling desires for reform through this approach will, at the least, be far off. Although fully articulated goals and standards are integral to reform, the urgency of reform also requires immediate action. Developing incentive plans, comparing the results of programs with their costs, and evaluating alternatives should all begin even before full agreement is reached on the details of subject matter standards and concomitant test instruments. Even with these latter developments, efficiency concerns and the use of performance incentives will remain important. Therefore, beginning reform centered on improving fundamental cognitive skills, which can currently be measured, even though imperfectly, is appropriate, useful, and necessary.

The Special Problems of Disadvantaged Students

Some policy discussions assume that all students and schools are more or less identical. At other times, disadvantaged populations are assumed to be completely distinct. Neither approach is appropriate, so a balance must be struck.

There is no reason to believe that the introduction of performance incentives and measurement would be either more or less important in central-city schools than in wealthy suburban schools. Nor is there any reason to believe that good teachers are less important in a rural setting than in a suburban or urban one. Yet disadvantaged students by definition face greater obstacles to achievement and pose greater problems to schools. They must learn despite the pressures of lower income and poorer housing. Moreover, disadvantaged students are also often hindered by poorly educated parents, an increased likelihood of having only one parent at home, and friends with low ambitions and scholastic performance. So the families of the disadvantaged are much less likely to make up for a bad schooling experience. Conversely, high-quality schooling is critically important for the performance of disadvantaged students who receive little encouragement in the home environment.

The special problems of disadvantaged students suggest the need for special, targeted policies to compensate for some of the specific disadvantages they face. Preschool programs, for example, might compensate for lower family inputs. Added health and nutrition programs, both for preschool children and for older children, may be another way to compensate for basic disadvantages. So might added counseling services at all ages. It is important, nonetheless, to subject these programs to regular performance measurement and evaluation, just as overall school programs are evaluated. Moreover, the programs should be structured to give participants—students, teachers, and other school personnel—direct performance incentives.

The Transition from School to Work

The current schooling system works best when preparing students for postsecondary education; it does much less well for students who either do not complete high school or who stop with a high school diploma. Schools are not held accountable for what happens to students after they leave, so it is not especially surprising that they have neither worked overly hard at ensuring the success of school-leavers nor tried hard to measure ex-students' success or lack thereof. Perhaps to a greater extent than in other areas of student performance, schools remain just one of many factors determining career success. Nevertheless, improving the skills that students bring to the workplace remains a primary motivation for the public's attention to schools, and schools cannot remain aloof as students leave to seek productive placement in society.

To resolve the problems of school-leavers, many have looked at education in other countries where school and work are often more closely linked. The German and Chinese schooling systems, for example, are both closely linked to apprenticeship programs in industry. Schools supply to specific firms and work to develop the skills needed by those firms. One characteristic of the schooling systems that are closely linked to work (and possibly further training) appears to be early identification and selection of students into a particular educational track. Students have more options for training and postsecondary education at later ages in the United States than in most other countries, but this extended opportunity apparently comes at the cost of rougher transitions for those who end schooling early.

The development of better school-to-work transitions within the American system calls for more contact between schools and employers, particularly in getting employers to define clearly their expectations for new employees. What skills are demanded? What shortcomings do employers see in current students? Direct feedback on the outcomes of schooling could suggest new goals for the schools to meet. This approach, concentrating on results, also differs significantly from much of the current effort to involve employers more actively in schools, an effort that is designed primarily to procure added financial support for school programs. Indeed, most dealings with schools are handled by a firm's community relations or public relations personnel rather than operations personnel. Financial support from the business community may be helpful in some specific situations, but it is unlikely to have a major influence on the educational system. More helpful would be closer relations between businesses and schools in determining the skills needed by business, designing systems to certify achievement of those skills, informing students of opportunities, and creating direct incentives for student achievement.

The Costs of Reform

Most reform proposals simply ignore the costs entailed, even though they make it absolutely clear that more resources will be required. We take a very different stance. We are unable to say whether the nation will, or should, pay more for the system that results from our suggested reforms. In the near term, however, the inefficient and often unproductive use of resources in today's schools suggests that schools could in general do a lot by redirecting existing spending to more productive uses. When that is done, but only when that is done, the nation may determine that it is spending enough on schools or it may decide to increase investment in schools. This is a question to be debated in the future, after fundamental changes have been instituted.

We take this position because we firmly believe that schools will improve only when they become better at making decisions to improve student performance. A real discipline can come from thinking of making change without raising costs—by eliminating ineffective policies and programs to make room for improvements. Schools are as unaccustomed to such discipline as they are to weighing the costs and effectiveness of programs, but they would benefit from both.

New Roles and Responsibilities

New organizations and incentives for schools will require everyone involved in education—from governments to students—to assume new roles and responsibilities.

Students and Parents

Most incentive systems for schools require more active decision-making by students and their parents. Any successful use of school choice obviously depends on the decisions made by parents and students in evaluating the quality of school programs. But students and parents must also take an active part in many other alternative systems. One line of promising new programs, including Accelerated Schools and others aimed at disadvantaged students, makes parent participation a key element. In any event, productive school reform will entail making more and better information available to parents, and the degree of success in reform will relate closely to what they do with this information. If they demand better schools, if they more actively participate in educational decisions, and if they evaluate schools' performance, parents can help forge a better school system.

State Governments

The most profound changes in our proposed reform will come at the level of state legislatures and state departments of education, which have the (state) constitutional authority and responsibility to provide for the education of their citizens. They do this by empowering local districts to organize and to operate schools. But states now force schools into a highly structured framework, which limits the freedom of local districts to adapt schooling to local conditions and which shows little explicit concern for student outcomes.

Virtually any significant reform of incentives for schools must redirect state policy. States will have to give local districts greater latitude to handle the difficulties associated with implementing fair and effective incentives and with increasing the involvement of teachers and administrators. The state's role should change to goal setting instead of management. Rather than create curricula and school programs, states should instead articulate goals for student achievement and facilitate achievement of those goals by local districts.

A particularly challenging aspect of this change is defining the goals that represent the central academic concerns of schools without making them so broad and diffuse as to be meaningless. Clear standards for performance in the main academic subjects are especially important. Strong political agendas tend to distort efforts to develop meaningful goals and standards, leading to two kinds of undesirable results. On the one hand, people who strongly believe that schools should instill children with moral and ethical values, good citizenship, and other laudable objectives press to include these as educational goals, which can make goals almost impossible to measure and to achieve. On the other hand, people concerned that their school will fail to meet current standards frequently press to lower the goals. This, for example, appears to be the history of the Regents' examinations in New York State, where previously high examination standards were lowered well below the standards of achievement already existing in many of the state's districts. Similar examples can be found in other states.

Identifying standards in core academic areas is proceeding, most notably in mathematics but also in other areas. The development of generally acclaimed mathematics standards has been the result of intensive efforts by mathematics teachers, researchers, users, and educational policymakers. States should support and participate in such efforts.

States also have a clear responsibility to establish a system of schooling that is conducive to high performance. The obvious way to encourage high performance is to create a system that rewards good performance. Although experience to draw upon is limited, establishing incentives based on outcomes appears superior to commonly used regulatory approaches. Such systems are radically different from the current organization of schooling, and moving to such a structure requires dramatic changes in outlook.

States should encourage local districts to experiment with incentive systems. A state might offer start-up grants for innovative programs, for example, or help disseminate new ideas, evaluate the results of local experiments, or establish cooperative arrangements with school districts to administer experiments.

The state should also reduce or eliminate restrictions on school districts that inhibit development of individually tailored and managed systems that emphasize performance. For example, current state certification and labor policies unnecessarily and unproductively constrain personnel policies of local districts. The standard undergraduate requirements for teachers, the common specifications of graduate education for teachers, and the rigidity of most teacher tenure regulations are examples of generally counterproductive regulations. All restrict options without promoting better student performance. Many of these restrictions grow out of desires to protect public employees, but employees are protected at the expense of students. A balance must be struck so that normal employee protections do not inhibit effective schooling.

Similarly, states frequently restrict the actual organization of classrooms and overall range of instructional approaches through regulations on class sizes, length of school days, curriculum and textbook choices, use of ancillary personnel in schools, provision of remedial programs, and the like. These frequently grow out of a distrust of the abilities or intentions of local districts and, perhaps, parents. But, in attempting to prevent the worst kinds of outcomes, states severely limit local choice and local involvement in devising educational approaches. Alternatives are needed for dealing with malfeasance or incompetence without simultaneously thwarting initiative.

Finally, state finance programs dictate both overall resources and their use. These programs frequently penalize districts for saving money or for organizing schools in nonstandard ways. Worse, they sometimes reduce or remove funds when student outcomes improve. It is simply not possible to encourage novel programs aimed at performance improvement while at the same time constraining schools so much that they have no flexibility in organization and behavior.

Concerns about local districts' abilities are legitimate. Many districts do not have the capacity to innovate. Moreover, some, if given the freedom, might implement obviously bad policies or greatly mismanage operations. They might, for example, downgrade academic performance in favor of other activities. The states should monitor the performance of local districts, particularly during experimentation with new policies and programs, and they should also redefine the role and activities of local school boards.

When a school district's performance does lag, however, the state should not impose even more regulations on the process of education, but should continue to concentrate on outcomes. When observed local outcomes are not acceptable, and when the state is convinced that the local district is not performing appropriately to improve these outcomes, the state should be prepared to ensure that the children of the district have alternative schooling opportunities. Such approaches exist in some form already. For example, the state of New Jersey has exercised its authority to manage local school districts when the local jurisdiction demonstrates an inability to meet minimal educational or financial management standards. Whether the takeover is successful depends on the ability of the state education department to hire more effective local school leaders. Other states have contemplated allowing children to go to other public or private schools when their public school is not meeting its objectives. This approach, which could be implemented by making full vouchers available in poorly performing districts, is more consistent with the student outcome-oriented approach stressed here. The students who have been ill served have an immediate chance to better their situation, a chance not dependent on the ability of new, external management to achieve a turnabout that was quick enough to matter.

States can also encourage innovation by helping local districts to manage experiments—by helping them both to design better experiments and to disseminate the results of experiments. The state department of education might, for example, develop an experimental branch responsible for designing and evaluating innovative programs. This approach has been applied with the STAR program in Tennessee, but only with limited scope and focus. The Tennessee program, for example, concentrated only on the effects of modestly lowered class sizes in early grades. But there is no reason why such limitations in focus could not be overcome. States could help to design different incentive structures, including ones that crossed district boundaries, such as wider school choice programs. Without some reforms by states—in particular a lessening of restrictive control from above and help in the evaluation of experiments—little learning about new organizations and incentives in schools will take place.

Federal Government

The federal government, which has never been the prime actor in elementary and secondary education, should change emphasis in many of its roles. It should take the lead in producing and distributing information about reforms, helping to set goals and standards, developing performance information, supporting broad program evaluation, and disseminating the results of evaluations. The federal government should also take major responsibility for developing and funding supplemental programs for disadvantaged and minority students. Because these programs involve meeting broad social goals concerning equality, leadership should rightfully emanate from the federal government. Evidence suggests that expansions of early childhood education, integrated health and nutrition programs, and other interventions to compensate for disadvantages of background may be particularly effective. Nonetheless, disadvantaged students will be aided first and foremost by improvements in the public schools already serving them or by expansion of alternative schooling opportunities. Improving core elementary and secondary education programs remains the single most effective way to improve the performance of disadvantaged students.

Local School Districts

Our proposed reforms would also bring substantial change to local school districts. They must take new responsibility for choosing curricula, managing teacher and administrative personnel (including hiring and firing, based on performance), and establishing closer links with businesses (particularly for students who are not continuing on to postsecondary schooling). Although none of these responsibilities is qualitatively different from the roles districts currently play, the devolution of greater decisionmaking authority from states to local authorities would require school districts to develop new and more capable management and leadership. Moreover, the governance of local districts requires special attention. Specifically, local school boards must concentrate on policy matters, not on the micromanagement of schools; the actual delivery of education should be left to the school professionals.

To improve performance, local schools must take a much more active role in decisionmaking about all aspects of the instructional program as well as the organizational structure of the school, rewards to personnel, and hiring and retention decisions for principals and teachers. Of course, local districts and schools will receive considerable information and guidance from state and federal education agencies, including guidance on goals, evaluation methods, organizational structures, and teaching approaches. School districts also will face a set of larger decisions, such as whether to contract for educational services or how to deal with alternative school proposals under charter school authority.

Each of these changes connects with all the others. A school system that generates and disseminates performance information enables students and parents to participate more confidently. Like school districts, parents will have to develop an ability to use better information in effective ways. As they become better decision-makers themselves, schools can help parents become involved.

Businesses

Although businesses have frequently deplored the quality of workers they receive from schools, they have never worked closely with schools to define the skills and abilities that they are looking for in prospective workers. If businesses were to provide more direct input to schools about requirements for students, perhaps coupled with long-term hiring relationships, schools, businesses, and the students would all be helped. Moreover, if businesses were to insist on high performance in school, showing interest in transcripts and other evidence of scholastic performance, students would have very different incentives to work hard in school. This approach, of course, presumes that businesses and schools can reach agreement on educational goals and desirable skills. A movement of schools into the realm of performance incentives puts them more in line with businesses, which have traditionally employed such incentives. Businesses might be helpful in developing systems of performance incentives for school personnel. Businesses could also help parents to become more involved in schools if, instead of providing monetary support for schools, they released time to their workers so that they could visit schools during the school day.

175

Comprehensive Reform

Promising programs for improving schools have been put forth almost since schools themselves were developed. Many have been tried; few have achieved even a modicum of success. Even the least successful often remain in practice, regardless of their ineffectiveness, because, with little evaluation of performance, schools have little incentive to disrupt the status quo. In some ways education's problem has been not too few ideas but too many ideas—none of them evaluated against standards of effectiveness.

This report does not advocate a specific organizational or incentive scheme. Instead it makes the case for an overall approach to reform. This approach stands on two pillars: incentives for high student performance, and a process of decisionmaking that weighs effectiveness of educational programs against their costs. Moreover, in addition to trying harder to distinguish programs that work from those that do not, schools must make widely known which programs have improved performance and why. This seems neither a controversial program for reform nor a complicated one: find out what works, tell everybody who will listen, and encourage them to do more of what works and less of what does not. This, the essence of any successful reform, has been ignored during decades of grandiose plans and programs. Without a mechanism for sorting out bad from good, prospects for reform are close to hopeless. That is what education must start to build, now.

Bibliographic Notes

For references on specific issues of incentives and evaluations, see notes in previous chapters. International performance on mathematics tests in 1991 is summarized in U.S. Department of Education (1993a). A good discussion of issues of school governance under altered incentives can be found in Committee for Economic Development (1994). The national goals along with the initial steps to implement them are contained in Goals 2000: Educate America Act (HR 1804), signed into law in April 1994.

Selected Bibliography

American Educational Research Association, American Psychological Association, and National Council on Measurement in Education. 1985. *Standards for Educational and Psychological Testing*. Washington: American Psychological Association.

American Federation of Teachers. n.d. *National Education Standards and Assessments*. Washington.

Amsler, Mary. 1992. "Charter Schools." Policy Briefs 19. Far Western Laboratory for Educational Research and Development, San Francisco.

Armor, David, and others. 1976. *Analysis of the School Preferred Reading Program in Selected Los Angeles Minority Schools*. Santa Monica, Calif.: Rand Corp.

Ashenfelter, Orley. 1987. "The Case for Evaluating Training Programs with Randomized Trials." *Economics of Education Review* 6 (4): 333–38.

Ballou, Dale, and Michael Podgursky. Forthcoming. "Recruiting Smarter Teachers." *Journal of Human Resources*.

Barnett, W. Steven. 1992. "Benefits of Compensatory Preschool Education." *Journal of Human Resources* 27 (Spring): 279–312.

Barnow, Burt S., and Glen G. Cain. 1977. "A Reanalysis of the Effect of Headstart on Cognitive Development: Methodology and Empirical Findings." *Journal of Human Resources* 12 (Spring): 177–97.

Barrett, Michael J. 1990. "The Case for More School Days." *Atlantic* 266 (November): 78–106.

Barro, Robert J. 1991. "Economic Growth in a Cross Section of Countries." *Quarterly Journal of Economics* 106 (May): 407–43.

Baumol, William J. 1967. "Macroeconomics of Unbalanced Growth: The Anatomy of Urban Crisis." *American Economic Review* 57 (June): 415–26.

Baumol, William J., and William G. Bowen. 1965. "On the Performing Arts: The Anatomy of Their Economic Problems." *American Economic Review* 55 (May): 495–502.

Becker, Gary S. 1975. *Human Capital: A Theoretical and Empirical Analysis, with Special Reference to Education*. 2d ed. New York: National Bureau of Economic Research.

Behrendt, Amy, Jeffrey A. Eisenach, and William R. Johnson. 1986. "Selectivity Bias and the Determinants of SAT Scores." *Economics of Education Review* 5 (4): 363–71.

Bennett, William J. 1988. *American Education: Making It Work: A Report to the President and the American People*. U.S. Department of Education.

Benson, Charles S., Maya H. H. Ibser, and Steven G. Klein. 1991. "Economic Returns to Vocational Education and Other Types of Occupational Training." PEER Background Paper.

Berrueta-Clement, John R., and others. 1984. *Changed Lives: The Effects of the Perry Preschool Program on Youths through Age 19.* Ypsilanti, Mich.: High/Scope Press.

Betts, Julian R. 1993. "Does School Quality Matter? Evidence from the National Longitudinal Survey of Youth." University of California, San Diego, Department of Economics.

Bishop, John. 1989. "Is the Test Score Decline Responsible for the Productivity Growth Decline?" *American Economic Review* 79 (March): 178–97.

———. 1991. "Achievement, Test Scores, and Relative Wages." In *Workers and Their Wages*, edited by Marvin H. Kosters, 146–86. Washington: AEI Press.

———. 1992. "The Impact of Academic Competencies on Wages, Unemployment, and Job Performance." *Carnegie-Rochester Conference Series on Public Policy* 37 (December): 127–94.

———. 1993. "Improving Job Matches in the U.S. Labor Market." *Brookings Papers on Economic Activity: Microeconomics: 1:* 335–90.

Boe, Erling E., and Dorothy M. Gilford, eds. 1992. *Teacher Supply, Demand, and Quality: Policy Issues, Models, and Data Bases: Proceedings of a Conference.* Washington: National Academy Press.

Bolick, Clint. 1994. "Puerto Rico: Leading the Way in School Choice." *Wall Street Journal,* January 14, A11.

Boozer, Michael A., Alan B. Krueger, and Shari Wolkon. 1992. "Race and School Quality since *Brown v. Board of Education." Brooking Papers on Economic Activity: Microeconomics*: 269–338.

Bound, John, and Richard B. Freeman. 1992. "What Went Wrong? The Erosion of Relative Earnings and Employment among Young Black Men in the 1980s." *Quarterly Journal of Economics* 107 (February): 201–32.

Breland, Hunter M. 1979. *Population Validity and College Entrance Measures.* New York: The College Board.

Callahan, Raymond E. 1962. *Education and the Cult of Efficiency: A Study of the Social Forces That Have Shaped the Administration of the Public Schools.* University of Chicago Press.

Cameron, Stephen V., and James J. Heckman. 1993. "The Nonequivalence of High School Equivalents." *Journal of Labor Economics* 11 (January, pt. 1): 1–47.

Card, David, and Alan B. Krueger. 1992a. "Does School Quality Matter? Returns to Education and the Characteristics of Public Schools in the United States." *Journal of Political Economy* 100 (February): 1–40.

———. 1992b. "School Quality and Black-White Relative Earnings: A Direct Assessment." *Quarterly Journal of Economics* 107 (February): 151–200.

Carnegie Foundation for the Advancement of Teaching. 1992. *School Choice: A Special Report.* Princeton, N.J.

Chaikind, Stephen, Louis C. Danielson, and Marsha L. Brauen. 1993. "What Do We Know about the Costs of Special Education? A Selected Review." *Journal of Special Education* 26 (4): 344–70.

Chubb, John E., and Terry M. Moe. 1990. *Politics, Markets, and America's Schools.* Brookings.

Clune, William H., and John F. Witte, eds. 1990. *Choice and Control in American Education*. Vol. 1: *The Theory of Choice and Control in Education*. Vol. 2: *The Practice of Choice, Decentralization, and School Restructuring*. New York: Falmer.

Cohen, David K., and Richard J. Murnane. 1985. "The Merits of Merit Pay." *Public Interest* 80 (Summer): 3–30.

———. 1986. "Merit Pay and the Evaluation Problem: Understanding Why Most Merit Pay Plans Fail and a Few Survive." *Harvard Education Review* 56 (February): 1–17.

Coleman, James S., and others. 1966. *Equality of Educational Opportunity*. U.S. Department of Health, Education, and Welfare.

Commission on the Skills of the American Workforce. 1990. *America's Choice: High Skills or Low Wages!* Rochester, N.Y.: National Center on Education and the Economy.

Committee for Economic Development. 1994. *Putting Learning First: Governing and Managing the Schools for High Achievement*. New York.

Congressional Budget Office. 1985. *Reducing Poverty among Children*.

———. 1986. *Trends in Educational Achievement*.

———. 1987. *Educational Achievement: Explanations and Implications of Recent Trends*.

Coons, John E., and Stephen D. Sugarman. 1978. *Education by Choice: The Case for Family Control*. Berkeley, Calif.: University of California Press.

Cornett, Lynn M., and Gale F. Gaines. 1994. "Reflecting on Ten Years of Incentive Programs: The 1993 SREB Career Ladder Clearinghouse Survey." Southern Regional Education Board, Atlanta.

Crouse, James, and Dale Trusheim. 1988. *The Case against the SAT*. University of Chicago Press.

Currie, Janet, and Duncan Thomas. 1993. "Does Head Start Make a Difference? NBER Working Paper 4406. Cambridge, Mass.: National Bureau of Economic Research. July.

Darlington, Richard B. 1980. "Preschool Programs and Later School Competency of Children from Low-Income Families." *Science,* April 11, 202–04.

Diegmueller, Karen. 1993a. "Charter-Schools Idea Gaining Converts in Legislatures." *Education Week*, July 14, p. 18.

——. 1993b. "Pennsylvania House Votes to Nullify State Board's Learner-Outcome Rules." *Education Week,* February 17, p. 19.

Dillon, Sam. 1994. "Teacher Tenure: Rights vs. Discipline." *New York Times,* June 28, pp. A1, B3.

Dunbar, Stephen B., and Elizabeth A. Witt. 1993. "Design Innovations in Measuring Mathematics Achievement." In *Measuring What Counts: A Conceptual Guide for Mathematics Assessment*, edited by National Research Council, Mathematical Sciences Education Board, 175–200. Washington: National Academy Press.

Dynarski, Mark. 1987. "The Scholastic Aptitude Test: Participation and Performance." *Economics of Education Review* 6 (3): 263–74.

Eberts, Randall W., and Joe A. Stone. 1984. *Unions and Public Schools: The Effect of Collective Bargaining on American Education.* Lexington, Mass.: Lexington Books.

——. 1985. "Wages, Fringe Benefits, and Working Conditions: An Analysis of Compensating Differentials." *Southern Economic Journal* 52 (July): 274–79.

Economist. 1993. "The Cash Street Kids." August 28, pp. 23–25.

Educational Testing Service. 1991. *Performance at the Top: From Elementary through Graduate School.* Princeton, N.J.

Ehrenberg, Ronald G., Randy A. Ehrenberg, and Richard P. Chaykowski. 1988. "Are School Superintendents Rewarded for 'Perfomance'?" In *Micro-Level School Finance: Issues and Implications for Policy*, edited by David H. Monk and Julie Underwood, 337–64. Cambridge, Mass.: Ballinger.

Farkas, George. 1993a. "Nine Propositions about Schooling, the Inheritance of Poverty, and Interventions to Reduce this Inheritance." School of Social Sciences, University of Texas at Dallas.

——. 1993b. "Structuring Tutoring for At Risk Children in the Early Years." *Applied Behavioral Science Review* 1 (1): 69–92.

Feldman, Joseph, and others. 1994. "Still Separate, Still Unequal: The Limits of Milliken II's Educational Compensation Remedies." Harvard Project on School Desegregation. April.

Ferguson, Ronald. 1991. "Paying for Public Education: New Evidence on How and Why Money Matters." *Harvard Journal on Legislation* 28 (Summer): 465–98.

Freeman, Richard B. 1986. "Unionism Comes to the Public Sector." *Journal of Economic Literature* 24 (March): 41–86.

Friedman, Milton. 1962. *Capitalism and Freedom.* University of Chicago.

Friend, Jamesine, Klaus Galda, and Barbara Searle. 1896. "From Nicaragua to Thailand: Adapting Interactive Radio Instruction." *Development Communication Report* 52 (Winter).

Friend, Jamesine, Barbara Searle, and Patrick Suppes, eds. 1980. *Radio Mathematics in Nicaragua.* Institute for Mathematical Studies in the Social Sciences, Stanford University.

Garden, Robert A. 1989. "Students' Achievements: Population B." In *The IEA Study of Mathematics II: Contexts and Outcomes of School Mathematics*, edited by David F. Robitaille and Robert A. Garden, 126–52. Oxford: Pergamon Press.

Garms, Walter I., James W. Guthrie, and Lawrence C. Pierce. 1978. *School Finance: The Economics and Politics of Public Education.* Prentice Hall.

General Accounting Office. 1993. *Student Testing: Current Extent and Expenditures, with Cost Estimates for a National Examination.* GAO/PEMD-93-8. January.

Gilford, Dorothy M., and Ellen Tenenbaum, eds. 1990. *Pre-College Science and Mathematics Teachers: Monitoring Supply, Demand, and Quality.* Washington: National Academy Press.

Glass, Gene V., and Mary Lee Smith. 1979. "Meta-Analysis of Research on Class Size and Achievement." *Educational Evaluation and Policy Analysis* 1 (1): 2–16.

Glenn, Charles L. 1989. *Choice of Schools in Six Nations: France, Netherlands, Belgium, Britain, Canada, West Germany.* Department of Education.

Goertz, Margaret E., Ruth B. Ekstrom, and Richard J. Coley. 1984. "The Impact of State Policy on Entrance into the Teaching Profession: Final Report." Educational Testing Service, Princeton, N.J. October.

Gramlich, Edward M. 1986. "Evaluation of Education Projects: The Case of the Perry Preschool Program." *Economics of Education Review* 5 (1): 17–24.

———. 1990. *A Guide to Benefit-Cost Analysis.* 2d ed. Prentice-Hall.

Gramlich, Edward M., and Patricia P. Koshel. 1975. *Educational Performance Contracting.* Brookings.

Grogger, Jeffrey. 1992. "Does School Quality Explain the Recent Black/White Wage Trend?" University of California at Santa Barbara, Department of Economics.

Grymes, John A., and Irene Baden Harwarth. 1992. *Historical Trends: State Education Facts, 1969 to 1989.* National Center for Education Statistics.

Hancock, Lynn, and Jeremy Kilpatrick. 1993. "Effects of Mandated Testing on Instruction." In *Measuring What Counts: A Conceptual Guide for Mathematics Assessment*, edited by National Research Council, Mathematical Sciences Education Board, 149–74. Washington: National Academy Press.

Hanushek, Eric A. 1971. "Teacher Characteristics and Gains in Student Achievement: Estimation Using Micro Data." *American Economic Review* 60 (May): 280–88.

———. 1976. "Comment." In *Education as an Industry*, edited by Joseph T. Froomkin, Dean T. Jamison, and Roy Radner, 191–96. Cambridge, Mass: Ballinger.

———. 1986. "The Economics of Schooling: Production and Efficiency in Public Schools." *Journal of Economic Literature* 24 (September): 1141–77.

———. 1989. "The Impact of Differential Expenditures on School Performance." *Educational Researcher* 18 (May): 45–51.

———. 1991. "Notes on School Finance 'Reform'." *PEER Background Paper.*

———. 1992. "The Trade-Off between Child Quantity and Quality." *Journal of Political Economy* 100 (February): 84–117.

———. 1993. "Can Equity Be Separated from Efficiency in School Finance Debates?" In *Essays on the Economics of Education*, edited by Emily P. Hoffman, 35–73. Kalamazoo, Mich.: W. E. Upjohn Institute for Employment Research.

183

———. 1994. "Money Might Matter Somewhere: A Response to Hedges, Laine, and Greenwald." *Educational Researcher* 23 (May): 5–8.

Hanushek, Eric A., and Richard R. Pace. Forthcoming. "Who Chooses to Teach (and Why)?" *Economics of Education Review*.

Hanushek, Eric A., and Steven G. Rivkin. 1994. "Understanding the 20th Century Explosion in U.S. School Costs." Working Paper 388. Rochester Center for Economic Research.

Hanushek, Eric A., and Richard Sabot. 1991. "Notes on Changes in Educational Performance." PEER Background Paper.

Hanushek, Eric A., and Lori L. Taylor. 1990. "Alternative Assessments of the Performance of Schools: Measurement of State Variations in Achievement." *Journal of Human Resources* 25 (Spring): 179–201.

Harp, Lonnie. 1993. "Pa. Parent Becomes Mother of 'Outcomes' Revolt." *Education Week*, September 22, pp. 19–21.

———. 1994. "In Cleveland, State Reaches $1 Million Accord to Keep Ohio Test." *Education Week,* June 1, p. 14.

Hartigan, John A., and Alexandra K. Wigdor, eds. 1989. *Fairness in Employment Testing: Validity Generalization, Minority Issues, and the General Aptitude Test Battery.* Washington: National Academy Press.

Hartman, William T. 1980. "Policy Effects of Special Education Funding Formulas." *Journal of Education Finance* 6 (Fall): 135–59.

Hatry, Harry P., John M. Greiner, and Brenda G. Ashford. 1994. *Issues and Case Studies in Teacher Incentive Plans.* 2d ed. Washington: Urban Institute.

Haveman, Robert H., and Barbara L. Wolfe. 1984. "Schooling and Economic Well-Being: The Role of Nonmarket Effects." *Journal of Human Resources* 19 (Summer): 377–407.

Hedges, Larry V., Richard D. Laine, and Rob Greenwald. 1994. "Does Money Matter? A Meta-Analysis of Studies of the Effects of Differential School Inputs on Student Outcomes." *Educational Researcher* 23 (April): 5–14.

184

Hill, Paul T., and Josephine Bonan. 1991. *Decentralization and Accountability in Public Education.* Santa Monica: RAND.

Hill, Russell C., and Frank Stafford. 1974. "Allocation of Time to Preschool Children and Educational Opportunity." *Journal of Human Resources* 9 (Summer): 323–41.

Holmes Group, The. 1986. *Tomorrow's Teachers: A Report of the Holmes Group.* East Lansing, Mich.

Hopfenberg, Wendy S., Henry M. Levin, and associates. 1993. *The Accelerated Schools Resource Guide.* San Francisco: Jossey-Bass Publishers.

Husén, Torsten, ed. 1967. *International Study of Achievement in Mathematics: A Comparison of Twelve Countries.* vol. 2. New York: John Wiley and Sons.

Jamison, Dean T. 1978. "Radio Education and Student Repetition in Nicaragua." In *The Radio Mathematics Project, Nicaragua, 1976–1977,* edited by Patrick Suppes, Barbara Searle, and Jamesine Friend. Stanford University, Institute for Mathematical Studies in the Social Sciences.

———. 1980. "Radio Education and Student Failure in Nicaragua: A Further Note." In *Radio Mathematics in Nicaragua,* edited by Jamesine Friend, Barbara Searle, and Patrick Suppes. Stanford University, Institute for Mathematical Studies in the Social Sciences.

Jamison, Dean T., and others. 1981. "Improving Elementary Mathematics Education in Nicaragua: An Experimental Study of the Impact of Textbooks and Radio on Achievement." *Journal of Educational Psychology* 73 (4): 556–67.

Johnson, Amy W., and Anita A. Summers. 1993 "What Do We Know about How Schools Affect the Labor Market Performance of Their Students?" EQW Working Paper. National Center on the Educational Quality of the Workforce. University of Pennsylvania.

Jorgenson, Dale W., and Barbara M. Fraumeni. 1992. "Investment in Education and U.S. Economic Growth." *Scandinavian Journal of Economics* 94 (Supplement): S51–S70.

Juhn, Chinhui, Kevin M. Murphy, and Brooks Pierce. 1991. "Accounting for the Slowdown in Black-White Wage Convergence."

In *Workers and Their Wages: Changing Patterns in the United States*, edited by Marvin H. Kosters, 107–43. Washington: AEI Press.

Juster, Thomas F., and Frank E. Stafford. 1991. "The Allocation of Time: Empirical Findings, Behavioral Models, and Problems of Measurement." *Journal of Economic Literature* 29 (June): 471–522.

Karnes, Elizabeth Lueder, and Donald D. Black. 1986. *Teacher Evaluation and Merit Pay: An Annotated Bibliography.* New York: Greenwood Press.

Kershaw, Joseph A., and Roland N. McKean. 1962. *Teacher Shortages and Salary Schedules.* McGraw-Hill.

Kiker, B. F. 1968. *Human Capital: In Retrospect.* University of South Carolina Press.

Kim, Hong-kyun. 1994. "Essays on the Behavior of Households' Human Capital Investments." Ph.D. dissertation, University of Rochester.

Kirsch, Irwin S., and others. 1993. *Adult Literacy in America: A First Look at the Results of the National Adult Literacy Survey.* Department of Education.

Koretz, Daniel M., and others. 1991. "The Effects of High-Stakes Testing on Achievement: Preliminary Findings about Generalization across Tests." Paper presented at American Educational Research Association meetings, April 5.

Koretz, Daniel M., and others. 1993a. *Interim Report: The Reliability of Vermont Portfolio Scores in the 1992–93 School Year.* Santa Monica, Calif.: RAND Institute on Education and Training.

Koretz, Daniel M., and others. 1993b. *The Vermont Portfolio Assessment Program: Findings and Implications.* Santa Monica, Calif.: RAND Institute on Education and Training.

Koretz, Daniel M., and others. 1993c. *Can Portfolios Assess Student Performance and Influence Instruction: The 1991–92 Vermont Experience.* CSE Technical Report 371, RAND Institute on Education and Training, Santa Monica, Calif.

Kosters, Marvin H. 1991. "Wages and Demographics." In *Workers and Their Wages: Changing Patterns in the United States*, edited by Marvin H. Kosters, 1–32. Washington: AEI Press.

Lankford, Hamilton, and James Wyckoff. 1993. "Where Has the Money Gone? An Analysis of School District Spending in New York, 1979–80 to 1991–92." In *Putting Children First.* vol. 2. Report prepared for the New York State Special Commission on Educational Structure, Policies, and Practices. Albany.

Lapointe, Archie E., Nancy A. Mead, and Gary W. Phillips. 1989. *A World of Difference: An International Assessment of Mathematics and Science.* Princeton, N.J.: Educational Testing Service.

Lau, Lawrence J., and Jong-Il Kim. 1992. "Human Capital and Aggregate Productivity: Some Empirical Evidence from the Group-of-Five Countries." Stanford University, Department of Economics, September 1992.

Leestma, Robert, and Herbert J. Walberg, eds. 1992. *Japanese Educational Productivity.* University of Michigan, Center for Japanese Studies.

Levin, Henry M. 1976. "Concepts of Economic Efficiency and Educational Production." In *Education as an Industry,* edited by Joseph T. Froomkin, Dean T. Jamison, and Roy Radner, 149–90. Cambridge, Mass.: Ballinger.

———. 1983a. *Cost Effectiveness: A Primer.* Beverly Hills, Calif.: Sage.

———. 1983b. "Cost Effectiveness in Evaluation Research." In *Handbook of Evaluation Research*, edited by Elmer L. Struening and Marcia Guttentag. vol. 2. Beverly Hills, Calif.: Sage.

———. 1991a. "The Economics of Educational Reforms for the Disadvantaged." PEER background paper.

———. 1991b. "Economics of Educational Time." PEER background paper.

———. 1993. "The Economics of Education for At-Risk Students." In *Essays on the Economics of Education*, edited by Emily P. Hoffman, 11–33. Kalamazoo, Mich.: W. E. Upjohn Institute for Employment Research.

———. 1994. "Learning from Accelerated Schools." In *School Improvement Programs: A Handbook for Educational Leaders*, edited by James H. Block, Susan T. Everson, and Thomas R. Guskey. New York: Scholastic Books.

Levin, Henry M., and Mun C. Tsang. 1987. "The Economics of Student Time." *Economics of Education Review* 6 (4): 357–64.

Levy, Frank, and Richard J. Murnane. 1992. "U.S. Earnings Levels and Earnings Inequality: A Review of Recent Trends and Proposed Explanations." *Journal of Economic Literature* 30 (September): 1333–81.

Lieberman, Myron. 1989. *Privatization and Educational Choice.* St. Martin's Press.

———. 1994. "The School Choice Fiasco." *Public Interest* 114 (Winter): 17–34.

Link, Charles R., and James G. Mulligan. 1986. "The Merits of a Longer School Day." *Economics of Education Review* 5 (1986): 373–81.

Lockheed, Marlaine E., and Eric A. Hanushek. 1988. "Improving Educational Efficiency in Developing Countries: What Do We Know?" *Compare* 18 (1): 21–38.

———. 1994. "Concepts of Educational Efficiency and Effectiveness." In *International Encyclopedia of Education*, edited by Torsten Husén and T. Neville Postlethwaite, 1779–83. 2d ed. vol. 3. Oxford: Pergamon Press.

Lucas, Robert E., Jr. 1988. "On the Mechanics of Economic Development." *Journal of Monetary Economics* 22 (July): 3–42.

McCarthy, Jane, and Suzanne Still. 1993. "Hollibrook Accelerated Elementary School." In *Restructuring Schooling: Learning from Ongoing Efforts*, edited by Joseph Murphy and Philip Hallinger, 63–83. Newbury Park, Calif.: Corwin Press.

McDonnell, Lorraine M., and Anthony Pascal. 1979. *Organized Teachers in American Schools.* Santa Monica, Calif.: RAND Corp.

McDonnell, Lorraine M., and Paul T. Hill. 1993. *Newcomers in American Schools: Meeting the Educational Needs of Immigrant Youth.* Santa Monica, Calif.: RAND Corp.

MacGuire, James. n.d. "Beyond Partisan Politics: A Response to the Carnegie Report on Choice." Center for Social Thought, New York.

McKnight, Curtis C., and others. 1987. *The Underachieving Curriculum: Assessing U.S. School Mathematics from an International Perspective*. Champaign, Ill.: Stipes Publishing Co.

McMillen, Marilyn M., and others. 1993. *Dropout Rates in the United States: 1992*. U.S. Department of Education.

Madden, Nancy A., and others. 1993. "Success for All: Longitudinal Effects of a Restructuring Program for Inner-City Elementary Schools." *American Educational Research Journal* 30 (Spring): 123–48.

Manski, Charles F. 1987. "Academic Ability, Earnings, and the Decision to Become a Teacher: Evidence from the National Longitudinal Study of the High School Class of 1972." In *Public Sector Payrolls*, edited by David A. Wise, 291–312. University of Chicago Press.

Marshall, Ray, and Marc Tucker. 1992. *Thinking for a Living: Education and the Wealth of Nations*. Basic Books.

Maynard, Rebecca, and Eileen McGinnis. 1991. "Policies to Meet the Need for High Quality Child Care." PEER background paper.

Medrich, Elliott A., and Jeanne E. Griffith. 1992. *International Mathematics and Science Assessments: What Have We Learned?* U.S. Department of Education.

Meyer, Robert H. 1993. "Can Schools Be Held Accountable for Good Performance? A Critique of Common Educational Performance Indicators." In *Essays on the Economics of Education*, edited by Emily P. Hoffman, 75–101. Kalamazoo, Mich.: W. E. Upjohn Institute for Employment Research.

Michael, Robert T. 1982. "Measuring Non-Monetary Benefits of Education: A Survey." In *Financing Education: Overcoming Inefficiency and Inequity*, edited by Walter W. McMahon and Terry G. Geske, 119–49. University of Illinois Press.

Monk, David H. 1990. *Educational Finance: An Economic Approach*. McGraw-Hill.

Montano, Jessie. 1989. "Choice Comes to Minnesota." In *Public Schools by Choice: Expanding Opportunities for Parents, Students, and Teachers*, edited by Joe Nathan, 165–80. St. Paul: Institute for Teaching and Learning.

189

Mosteller, Frederick, and Daniel Patrick Moynihan, eds. 1972. *On Equality of Educational Opportunity*. Random House.

Moynihan, Daniel Patrick. 1986. *Family and Nation*. Harcourt Brace Jovanovich.

Murnane, Richard J. 1975. *Impact of School Resources on the Learning of Inner City Children*. Cambridge, Mass: Ballinger.

———. 1991. "Evidence on Teacher Supply and Directions for Policy." PEER background paper.

Murnane, Richard J., and Frank Levy. 1992. "Education and Training." In *Setting Domestic Priorities: What Can Government Do?*, edited by Henry J. Aaron and Charles L. Schultze, 185–222. Brookings.

Murnane, Richard J., and Barbara Phillips. 1981. "What Do Effective Teachers of Inner-City Children Have in Common?" *Social Science Research* 10 (March): 83–100.

Murnane, Richard J., John B. Willett, and Frank Levy. 1993. "The Growing Importance of Cognitive Skills in Wage Determination." Harvard University, Graduate School of Education.

Murnane, Richard J., and others. 1991. *Who Will Teach? Policies That Matter*. Harvard University Press.

Murphy, Kevin M., and Finis Welch. 1989. "Wage Premiums for College Graduates: Recent Growth and Possible Explanations." *Educational Researcher* 18 (May): 17–26.

———. 1991. "The Role of International Trade in Wage Differentials." In *Workers and Their Wages: Changing Patterns in the United States*, edited by Marvin H. Kosters, 39–69. Washington: AEI Press.

———. 1992. "The Structure of Wages." *Quarterly Journal of Economics* 107 (February): 285–326.

Nathan, Joe. 1989a. "Progress, Problems, and Prospects with State Choice Plans." In *Public Schools by Choice: Expanding Opportunities for Parents, Students, and Teachers*, edited by Joe Nathan, 203–24. St. Paul: Institute for Learning and Teaching.

Nathan, Joe, and James Ysseldyke. 1994. "What Minnesota Has Learned about School Choice." *Phi Delta Kappan* 75 (May): 682–88.

National Board for Professional Teaching Standards. 1991. *Toward High and Rigorous Standards for the Teaching Profession.* 3d ed. Detroit.

National Council on Education Standards and Testing. 1992. *Raising Standards for American Education.* Department of Education.

National Education Commission on Time and Learning. 1994. *Prisoners of Time.* U.S. Department of Education.

National Research Council, Mathematical Sciences Education Board. 1993. *Measuring What Counts: A Conceptual Guide for Mathematics Assessment.* Washington: National Academy Press.

Nelson, F. Howard. 1991. *International Comparison of Public Spending on Education.* Washington: American Federation of Teachers, Research Department.

Newhouse, Joseph P. 1992. "Medical Care Costs: How Much Welfare Loss?" *Journal of Economic Perspectives* 6 (Summer): 3–21.

O'Day, Jennifer A., and Marshall S. Smith. 1993. "Systemic School Reform and Educational Opportunity." In *Designing Coherent Education Policy: Improving the System,* edited by Susan Fuhrman, chap. 8. Jossey-Bass.

Office of Technology Assessment. 1988. *Power On! New Tools for Teaching and Learning.* Washington: Government Printing Office.

———. 1992. *Testing in American Schools: Asking the Right Questions.* Washington: Government Printing Office.

O'Neill, Dave M., and Peter Sepielli. 1985. *Education in the United States: 1940–1983.* Department of Commerce.

O'Neill, June. 1990. "The Role of Human Capital in Earnings Differences between Black and White Men." *Journal of Economic Perspectives* 4 (Fall): 25–45.

Organization for Economic Co-operation and Development (OECD). 1992. *Education at a Glance: OECD Indicators.* Paris.

———. 1993. *Education at a Glance: OECD Indicators.* Paris.

Owen, Linda. 1993. "Students Find School Choice Proliferating in Minnesota." *Saint Paul Pioneer Press,* December 1, pp. 1C, 3C.

Pauly, Edward. 1991. *The Classroom Crucible: What Really Works, What Doesn't, and Why.* Basic Books.

Pennsylvania State Board of Education. 1993. "Rules and Regulations: Title 22–Education." *Pennsylvania Bulletin* 23 (July 24): 3549–65.

Randall, Ruth E. 1992. "What Comes after Choice?" *Executive Educator* (October): 35–38.

Ravitch, Diane. 1994. *National Standards and Assessment in American Education*. Brookings.

Ravitch, Diane, and Chester E. Finn, Jr. 1987. *What Do Our 17-Year-Olds Know? A Report on the First National Assessment of History and Literature*. Harper and Row.

Rivkin, Steven G. 1991. "Residential Segregation and School Integration." PEER background paper.

Romer, Paul. 1990. "Endogenous Technological Change." *Journal of Political Economy* 98 (October, pt. 2): S71–S102.

Rothman, Robert. 1993. "Amid Controversy, Pa. Board Adopts 'Learner Outcomes'." *Education Week*, January 20, p. 14.

Rumberger, Russell W. 1987. "The Impact of Salary Differentials on Teacher Shortages and Turnover: The Case of Mathematics and Science Teachers." *Economics of Education Review* 6 (4): 389–99.

Sabot, Richard, and Richard Freeman. 1991. "Test Scores and Labor Productivity." PEER background paper.

Salganik, Laura Hersh, and others. 1993. *Education in States and Nations: Indicators Comparing U.S. States with the OECD Countries in 1988*. Department of Education.

Schmidt, Peter. 1994. "Private Enterprise." *Education Week*, May 25, pp. 27–30.

Schultz, Theodore W. 1963. *The Economic Value of Education*. Columbia University Press.

Schweinhart, Lawrence J., Helen V. Barnes, and David P. Weikart. 1993. *Significant Benefits: The High/Scope Perry Preschool Study through Age 27*. Ypsilanti, Mich.: High/Scope Press.

Scitovsky, Tibor, and Anne Scitovsky. 1959. "What Price Economic Progress?" *Yale Review* 49 (Autumn): 95–110.

Shanker, Albert. 1993. "Achieving High Standards." Address to the 1993 QuEST Conference, Washington. July.

———. 1994 "Standards in Ohio." *New York Times*, May 1, p. E7.

Singer, Judith D., and John A. Butler. 1987. "The Education for All Handicapped Children Act: Schools as Agents of Social Reform." *Harvard Education Review* 57 (May): 125–52.

Slavin, Robert E., and others. 1990. "Success for All: First-Year Outcomes of a Comprehensive Plan for Reforming Urban Education." *American Educational Research Journal* 27 (Summer): 255–78.

Smith, Adam. 1979 [1776]. *An Inquiry into the Nature and Causes of the Wealth of Nations*. Reprint. Oxford: Clarendon Press.

Smith, James P., and Finis R. Welch. 1989. "Black Economic Progress after Myrdal." *Journal of Economic Literature* 27 (June): 519–64.

Smith, Marshall S., and Jennifer O'Day. 1990. "Systemic School Reform." In *The Politics of Curriculum and Testing*, edited by Susan Fuhrman and Batty Malen, 233–67. New York: Falmer.

Snyder, Thomas D., ed. 1993. *120 Years of American Education: A Statistical Portrait*. U.S. Department of Education.

Solmon, Lewis C., and Cheryl L. Fagnano. 1991. "Business and University Collaboration with the Schools." PEER background paper.

Solmon, Lewis C., and Steven G. Rivkin. 1991. "The Demography of American Education into the Next Century." PEER background paper.

Steuerle, C. Eugene, Robert H. Meyer, and Eric A. Hanushek. 1991. "Bringing Educational Measurement into the Age of Newton." *Policy Bites* 9 (October): 1–4.

Stevenson, Harold W., Shing-Ying Lee, and James W. Stigler. 1986. "Mathematics Achievement of Chinese, Japanese, and American Children." *Science*, February 14, pp. 693–99.

Stevenson, Harold W., and James W. Stigler. 1992. *The Learning Gap: Why Our Schools Are Failing and What We Can Learn from Japanese and Chinese Education*. New York: Summit Books.

Strauss, Robert P. 1993. *Who Should Teach in Pennsylvania's Public Schools?* Carnegie-Mellon University, Center for Public Financial Management.

———. 1994. "Teacher Certification Tests and the Personnel Decision." In *Education Management Guidelines*, 1–3. Pennsylvania School Boards Association. Harrisburg. April.

Sturm, Roland. 1993. *How Do Education and Training Affect a Country's Economic Performance?* Santa Monica, Calif.: RAND Corp.

Summers, Anita A., and Amy W. Johnson. 1994. "A Review of the Evidence on the Effects of School-Based Management Plans." PEER background paper.

Task Force on Teaching as a Profession. 1986. *A Nation Prepared: Teachers for the 21st Century.* Washington: Carnegie Forum on Education and the Economy.

U.S. Bureau of the Census. 1975. *Historical Statistics of the United States, Colonial Times to 1970, Bicentennial Edition.* vols. 1, 2. U.S. Department of Commerce.

U.S. Department of Education, National Center for Education Statistics, Information Services. 1993a. *The Condition of Education 1993.*

———. 1993b. *Federal Support for Education: Fiscal Years 1980 to 1993.*

Weaver, W. Timothy. 1983. *America's Teacher Quality Problem: Alternatives for Reform.* Praeger.

Weimer, David L., and Aidan R. Vining. 1992. *Policy Analysis: Concepts and Practice.* 2d ed. Prentice Hall.

Williams, Scott, and Mark Buechler. 1993. "Charter Schools." Policy Bulletin PB-B16, Indiana University, Indiana Education Policy Center.

Wirtz, Willard, and others. 1977. *On Further Examination: Report of the Advisory Panel and the Scholastic Aptitude Test Score Decline.* New York: College Entrance Examination Board.

Witte, John F., Andrea B. Bailey, and Christopher A. Thorn. 1993. "Third-Year Report: Milwaukee Parental Choice Program." University of Wisconsin, La Follette Institute of Public Affairs.

Woellner, Elizabeth H. 1982. *Requirements for Certification, 1982–83.* University of Chicago Press.

Wolfe, Barbara L., and Sam Zuvekus. 1991. "Nonmarket Outcomes of Schooling." PEER background paper.

Word, Elizabeth, and others. 1990. *The State of Tennessee's Student/Teacher Achievement Ratio (Project STAR), Final Summary Report*. Nashville: Tennessee State Department of Education.

World Bank. 1993. *The East Asian Miracle: Economic Growth and Public Policy*. New York: Oxford University Press.

Zerbe, Richard O., Jr., and Dwight D. Dively. 1994. *Benefit-Cost Analysis in Theory and Practice*. Harper Collins College Publishers.